CHANGING MINDSETS OF EDUCATIONAL LEADERS TO IMPROVE SCHOOLS

Voices of Doctoral Students

Edited by
Sandra Harris

Rowman & Littlefield Education
Lanham, Maryland • Toronto • Oxford
2005

Published in the United States of America
by Rowman & Littlefield Education
A Division of Rowman & Littlefield Publishers, Inc.
A wholly owned subsidiary of The Rowman & Littlefield Publishing Group, Inc.
4501 Forbes Boulevard, Suite 200, Lanham, Maryland 20706
www.rowmaneducation.com

PO Box 317
Oxford
OX2 9RU, UK

Copyright © 2005 by Sandra Harris

All rights reserved. No part of this publication may be reproduced, stored in a retrieval system, or transmitted in any form or by any means, electronic, mechanical, photocopying, recording, or otherwise, without the prior permission of the publisher.

British Library Cataloguing in Publication Information Available

Library of Congress Cataloging-in-Publication Data

Changing mindsets of educational leaders to improve schools : voices of doctoral students / [ed. by] Sandra Harris.
    p. cm.
 Includes bibliographical references and index.
 ISBN 1-57886-255-8 (pbk. : alk. paper)
 1. Educational leadership. 2. School improvement programs. 3. Education—Aims and objectives. I. Harris, Sandra, 1946–
  LB2831.6.C43 2005
  371.2—dc22
                                    2005000060

∞™ The paper used in this publication meets the minimum requirements of American National Standard for Information Sciences—Permanence of Paper for Printed Library Materials, ANSI/NISO Z39.48-1992.
Manufactured in the United States of America.

CONTENTS

Introduction   v

1   Ethical Leadership with Moral Purpose and Courage: When the Concept of Right and Wrong Is Not Enough   1
Debra Mahfouz Jordan

2   Research, Reflection, and Relationships: Discovering the 3 Rs of Teacher-Leaders   11
Gary Clarke

3   Practice to Passion   21
Delinda Neal

4   One Educator's Journey: Getting on Board the Change Train toward a Culture of Success   28
Stephen D. Patterson

5   From Teaching to Reaching: Caring as an Instructional Imperative   37
Jeffrey R. Schultz

6   Making Education Count   47
Linda Bass

7	Successful or Significant? The Role of Educational Grace Jim Vaszauskas	55
8	My Journey on the Yellow Brick Road Sharon Young	65
9	Empowerment: The Quickening Logan Faris	75
10	Inclusion: Some Social Justice Issues Sharon Kathleen Ninness	83
11	Choosing to Change Terri R. Hebert	96
12	Out of Cultural Bondage into the Promised Land of Cultural Diversity Paul Vickers	104
13	Unlocking the Gates: Entering the Realm of Understanding Sherry Durham	113
14	The Metamorphosis of Caring Nelda Wellman	123
15	My Story, My Song: Reflections Inspired by the Process Perry Daniel	131
16	Spirituality: Anchor of Leadership Wendell Wellman	140
17	A Recursive Process of Changing Paradigms in Doctoral Education Leadership Programs Betty Alford	150
18	Changing Mindsets of Educational Leaders Sandra Harris	159
References		166
Index		175

INTRODUCTION

> Over the last few years, a national conversation has emerged around the issue of educational leadership.
>
> —Michelle Young, NCAELP Report, 2001

In 1987, the National Commission on Excellence in Educational Administration concluded that educational leadership preparation programs in the United States were marked by a "lack of a definition of good educational leadership . . . lack of collaboration between school districts and universities . . . and lack of . . . modern content, and clinical experiences" (Milstein & Krueger, 1997, p. 101). Use of isolated theories and management models from the social sciences were no longer relevant to the primary need of today's schools. Starratt (2004) reiterated this theme when he wrote about his own experiences that "graduate schools were still mired in the dominant positivism of the social sciences with a little seasoning of a rather polite politics of administration" (p. 261).

Criticism that graduate programs are not bridging the gap between scholarly theory and practice has been the catalyst for reexamining master's and doctoral programs "to meet the needs of the society of the 21st century" (Nyquist & Woodford, 2000, p. 2). Many scholars in the field, most notably Joseph Murphy (1999), have argued for a programmatic change that emphasizes teaching and learning under the umbrella of school improvement. In the fall of 2000, a national panel of representatives from practice, preparation, professional development, and policy met to collaboratively consider the status of educational leadership. The following year, the National Commission for the Advancement of Educational Leadership Preparation (NCAELP) was established. The challenge to NCAELP is to examine and improve the quality of educational leadership preparation in the United States.

By identifying appropriate structures and pedagogical approaches for understanding and developing student knowledge, skills, and dispositions, doctoral learning has often resulted in a redesign of structure and pedagogy of administrator preparation programs. Some of these components have been an increased use of problem-based learning, cohort groups, collaborative partnerships between university and school district, internships or field experiences, and better use of technology in program delivery and content. Examples of innovative doctoral programs that prepare district administrators include (Jackson & Kelley, 2001):

- Hofstra University implemented a cohort with students beginning with the certification program in the first two years. A doctoral-only sequence includes a yearlong team-taught course on doctoral work, methods of inquiry, and a general overview of the historical research of the field. The next two years focus on projects and research strands.
- Fordham University implemented a cohort program with a sequence of courses planned over a two-year period and the dissertation taking the next two to four years to complete for an Ed.D. Completion rates have reached 80% with students completing in less than five years.
- Miami University (Ohio) focuses on the development of intellectual, moral, and technical practice. Critical reflection on present practices informed by theoretical knowledge with a problem-based approach is emphasized.

The dialogue to redefine and recenter educational leadership programs continues to lead to a reenvisioning process where preparation

INTRODUCTION

programs have redefined what an "'intellectual' is and does" (Mullen, 2003, p. 5) within the framework of being a scholar and a practitioner. Often, leadership programs designed to bridge this gap are referred to as scholar-practitioner programs. Their coursework tends to emphasize reculturing schools through curriculum and instructional leadership, school change, democratic community, diversity, social justice, and field-based activities. Starratt (2004) points out that in this setting, university professors are engaged in building a bridge between critical scholars and theorists to become "bridge scholars who can effectively carry that critique closer to the practice of teaching and learning and the practice of leading schools" (p. 265).

Vanderbilt University, for example, follows the scholar-practitioner model and emphasizes developing the "capacity of students to apply current theories from sociology, economics, political science to problems of practice" (http://peabody.vanderbilt.edu). Professors at Rowan University pointed out that their doctoral program should focus on leadership, not administration, and that it should have a visionary focus, be oriented toward effecting change, promote risk taking, and be problem oriented while integrating theory with practice (http://www.rowan.edu/selfstudy/four.html).

Educational leadership programs are being restructured to better balance the role of scholar and practitioner to one that is scholar-practitioner; they are also growing in number, making advanced study more accessible to students. For example, Texas has approximately 20 doctoral programs, with several more in the planning stages, yet 20 years ago there were only 4 or 5. Today in the United States, there are nearly 200 doctoral programs in educational leadership (http://www.alleducation-schools.com).

The educational leadership program at Stephen F. Austin State University (SFA), a regional university in Texas, has one of these new doctoral programs. The emphasis of this cohort program is that of preparing students to be scholar-practitioners who will have the knowledge and skills to improve schools. The 16 essays in this book are written by a cohort of doctoral students who share their personal stories of how this approach is affecting their practice. Also included is a chapter by Dr. Betty Alford that synthesizes some of the experiences of previous students who have participated in the SFA program.

The doctoral students were asked to develop a 10–12 page paper that reflected on prior doctoral readings and discussions and addressed their changing identity regarding a primary educational topic of leadership, such as social justice, change, or empowerment, and so forth. They were asked to critically address the following issues:

- Who I was (this is what I believed)
- What my practice looked like (this is what I did)
- Who I am now (this is what I believe now)
- What my practice looks like now (this is what I do now)
- Who I want to be (this is how my beliefs continue to change)
- What my practice will look like (this is what I envision doing)

Much of the dialogue of the "national conversation" regarding educational leadership centers on a two-pronged question: As students learn about leadership, does this change their practice? If so, does this changing practice result in school improvement? The essays in this book suggest that students participating in a doctoral program do change their leadership practices and, in doing so, they improve schools. The following student essays and the essay by Dr. Betty Alford, who is currently department chair in this particular scholar-practitioner program, describe the changes that reconstruct students' leadership mindsets to improve schools . . . and in the process to improve their own lives.

1

ETHICAL LEADERSHIP WITH MORAL PURPOSE AND COURAGE: WHEN THE CONCEPT OF RIGHT AND WRONG IS NOT ENOUGH

Debra Mahfouz Jordan

> [A]n educational leader who promotes the success of all students by acting with integrity, fairness, and in an ethical manner [is] a champion for children.
>
> —State Board for Educator Certification Superintendent Standard

In the rich tapestry of my early childhood, I became an ethical being. How this ethicality evolved is a story within itself. To simplify the process, I can tell you that some of my earliest memories are of Sunday school Bible stories and of adults reading me stories where the villains were big, bad wolves and the heroes were easily identifiable by their supernatural abilities with an uncanny sense of timing that allowed them to rush in and save the day. As a child, I saved my grandmother by cutting the bad wolf out of my storybook and throwing him away. I can vividly remember walking down a dusty driveway in southeast Texas to get a replica of my favorite cartoon character out of the mailbox—Mighty Mouse. What commonalities do Bible stories, big bad wolves, and an opera-singing, flying mouse share with the role I occupy today as a principal and an educational leader? In today's challenging educational arena, educational leaders have to possess the ability to recognize the villains and the heroes, have an impeccable sense of timing, and possess an unshakeable moral purpose. They must be heroes and champions for children.

ESTABLISHING THE VISION OF AN EDUCATIONAL HERO

Historically, American society has looked to the schools to help it achieve dreams for its children and for the nation. Recently, the metaphor of hero was attached to educational leaders—"leaders who personify the culture's values and as such provided tangible role models" (Deal & Kennedy, 1982, p. 14). Explaining this concept further, Deal and Kennedy developed a picture of an educational leader-hero as a "pivotal figure in a strong culture, the great motivator, the magician, the person everyone will count on when things get tough" (p. 37). Is this a realistic metaphor for an educational leader? Along with all of the hats we have to wear as educational leaders, are we now supposed to don a cape?

Shedding additional insight on the heroic metaphor, Fullan (2003) noted that this hero was not "a band of noblesse oblige do-gooders roaming the street and countryside blessing the downtrodden with their wisdom" (p. 59). This person was an educational leader imbued with respect, competence, and personal regard for others interlaced with morality and integrity (Bryk & Schneider, 2003). These heroes were mere humans who utilized their own distinct personalities and abilities to establish a climate of respect and care, demonstrating that success lies within human capacity, and ultimately transforming individual lives, classrooms, schools, and our societies. Better yet, these heroes could be school principals who lead with ethics, moral purpose, and courage to create socially just schools.

CONSTRUCTING AN EDUCATIONAL LEADER AS AN ETHICAL HERO

During my studies at the doctoral level, I discovered that Starratt (1991) believed that the constructivist theory suggested that humans constructed knowledge through the constructions of many humans over time until ultimately this knowledge became a diverse, multidimensional, ever-changing product that expanded as humanity evolved. Synthesizing this process of constructing, deconstructing, and reconstructing knowledge with the complexities of ethical leadership created a path that required achieving a balance between my personal beliefs and the behaviors I engaged in as a principal. It was also during this time that I read Kidder's (1996) insights on ethical dilemmas, Starratt's (1991) notion of schools as ethical institutions, and Greenfield's (1987) definition of deliberately moral administrators.

Synthesizing the knowledge I had gained with my practice as an educational leader, many times I acknowledged that I had struggled with issues that did not have clear-cut answers—dilemmas that required soul-searching and reflection, and still left a feeling of dissonance—while other times I dealt with issues swiftly and decisively. As I questioned this paradox, and I delved into the subject of ethical dilemmas and ethical decision making, I encountered a level of complexity that I had not thought about before, and this changed the way that I viewed these scenarios, and the way that I resolved them. Along the way, the experiences I encountered as a doctoral student and a member of a cohort strengthened and added a different dimension to this topic. A more complex level of ethical choice became evident—moral duty that manifested itself in everyday decisions concerning student achievement, curriculum, discipline, and policy.

Through my educational journey, I recognized that I had reconstructed the very basis of ethical choice from maintaining and sustaining personal ethics in a challenging educational climate to accepting the responsibility of creating an ethical institution (Starratt, 1991). Additionally, this ethical institution would include dialogues concerning Dewey's principles of democracy, social justice, and equity. As I read and engaged in dialogue concerning ethics, moral purpose, and courage, I realized the immense challenge for an educational leader to be "heroic"—a champion for our students, teachers, and the community.

MEETING THE CHALLENGE OF ETHICAL LEADERSHIP

John Moulton (1924) defined ethics as "obedience to the unenforceable" (p. 1). Duffy (2003) asserted that ethics referred to moral choice between right and wrong concerning truth and justice. Building on the relevance of right and wrong, truth and justice, Bullard and Taylor (1993) noted, "America's children have entrusted us with their dreams. They come to us able, brave and willing. We are the stewards of their future, as they are of ours" (p. 410). Our forefathers began a legacy where "education in the United States has a strong tradition, at least in rhetoric, of liberalism and democracy, wherein notions of opportunity and equality have been central values" (Groves, 2002, p. 16).

Thus, as educational leaders, it is a moral imperative to recognize the culture of the school arenas and ensure our rhetoric of democracy becomes a reality for all of our students. As a principal, I cannot be guilty of silencing and marginalizing groups of people because they do not meet the norm of the dominant culture (Anderson, 1998). Neither should I allow the current educational climate to destroy the creativity and imagination of our teachers and students, thus destroying the collective creativity of the group (Greenfield, 1987). However, in this arena of school reform and state-mandated test scores, moral leadership will have to achieve a balance between the needs of the students and the political demands of high-stakes testing. Duffy (2003) questioned this relationship between ethics and politics noting a "paradox created in the minds of some people" (p. 11). How do educational leaders address this paradox?

As a seasoned administrator, I have years of experience with accountability and testing. I was taught and I embraced the philosophy that whether we believed in testing or not, it was the only game in town and our students had to be able to compete. Campus decisions and campus planning all centered on the mission of improving student achievement—higher test scores. However, during the summer school on my campus, I witnessed four third-graders take the TAKS reading test for the "final" time. The test coordinator was looking for TAKS pencils, and one of the elementary principals brought the students lucky pennies. The stress and anxiety was palpable, and the adults giving the test expressed their concerns about the students, especially the one who had already cried. As I reflected on this experience during the day and later that evening, I questioned the process that required eight-year-old children to take the final version of a reading test that would determine if they passed or failed third grade, and I questioned my own role in this process.

As a principal with a competitive nature, of a seventh- and eighth-grade campus, I am actively engaged in raising test scores on the campus, and I have loved the process—the "thrill of victory and the agony of defeat." However, I will never make another decision about accountability and testing in the same manner. I will never forget the toll that unchecked accountability is taking on our children, teachers, and parents or fail to recognize the moral purpose required to achieve a healthy balance when addressing the dilemmas that are so prevalent in the today's troubled times.

Fullan (2003) noted, "One of the greatest strengths one needs in troubled times, is a strong sense of moral purpose . . . of the highest order . . . where all students learn, the gap between high and low performance becomes greatly reduced, and what people learn enables them to be successful citizens and workers in a morally based knowledge society" (p. 29). Thus as educational leaders, we must wrestle with what it means to be moral leaders who embody justice and caring, and demonstrate a genuine concern for the development of others.

POSSESSING THE MORAL PURPOSE TO RESOLVE THE DILEMMAS

Reflecting on my practice as a school principal revealed that there were dilemmas, where the conflict seemed to last longer and take the energy away from the primary mission of the school—learning. Daily I had to determine the consequences to students who broke the discipline code. Did I mete out justice, or did I mitigate the consequences with mercy? Did I deny an at-risk student's credits for failing to meet compulsory attendance standards, or did I accept extenuating circumstances? Did I place a student in a discipline-based alternative educational placement, or did I work to keep the student in the regular classroom? How did I balance the needs of one with the needs of many? Did I work with a marginal probationary employee, or did I recommend nonrenewal? Did I support a teacher's decision even though I did not believe it was in the best interest of the student? These were decisions that were polarizing in nature, and no matter which way I chose, someone would be unhappy. How did I resolve these dilemmas? How was I going to live with these decisions and justify them to others and myself? What ethical guidelines or moral compass would guide me to make the best decision, and how did I determine what was best for whom?

Kidder (1996) provided insight into these dilemmas when he divided ethical decision making into two categories—right versus wrong and right versus right. In the right versus wrong choices, the moral choice is usually clear and involves matters of law, truth, or morality. This is in contrast to right versus right, which creates the complex dilemmas, and which can be divided into four paradigms:

- truth versus loyalty, where issues of personal honesty or integrity come in conflict with responsibility, allegiance, and promise keeping;
- individual versus community, in which the interests of the individual are lined up against those of a larger entity;
- short term vs. long term, where the real and important concerns of the present are pitted against foresight and investment for the future;
- justice vs. mercy, in which fairness and an equal application of the rules appear to be at odds with the demands of empathy and compassion. (Kidder, 2002, p. 3)

Applying Kidder's (1996) four paradigms into my practice as a principal revealed that as an educational leader, I am exposed to this type of decision making daily. In my world, it is right to demonstrate loyalty and support to the teachers in their efforts to educate and teach students responsibility. It is right to have high standards and to expect students to come to class prepared with all homework done. However, is it right to have a "no late work" policy that penalizes students who come from economically disadvantaged homes, with little or no parental support with homework and school supplies? What does a zero on an assignment teach a seventh- or eighth-grade student? What does a "zeroes aren't permitted" program teach these same students?

Another scenario that depicts ethical dilemmas concerns decisions that are made based on preserving the order or safety of the larger school community versus the needs of an individual. When I am working with a first-year teacher on the campus, and this teacher shows a lack of judgment concerning the welfare of students and a lack of commitment to teaching on several occasions, do I renew the teaching contract? Is my primary responsibility to the teacher or to the students? What if the teacher loves students and teaching? It is the right thing to expect quality teaching and sound decision making in every classroom. It is equally right to coach, mentor, and develop young educators.

Third, as educational leaders cope with the demands of high-stakes testing in a changing and diverse society, the issue of short-term gains versus long-term benefits emerges. Starratt (1991) asserted that some people benefit at the expense of others in every social arrangement; to assume that school is always just is "ethically naive, if not culpable" (p. 1). As leaders, educators have the responsibility to create and maintain ethical organizations. How do I, as a principal, function in this system that demands achievement and groups and labels children in so many ways—minority, economically disadvantaged, at-risk, special education, English as a Second Language, gifted and talented . . . ? What effect will these decisions have on these groups of students? How are these placements determined? What educational opportunities are afforded to these groups? As an educator, it is ethical to meet the individual educational needs of every student. Is it ethical if the students are caught in the web of social administration, and often categorized and labeled on the basis of mistaken perceptions and assumptions? As a principal, I have to answer these questions and make decisions that promote and foster equal educational opportunities for all learners.

Finally, as I reflected on decisions concerning mercy versus justice, my thoughts were drawn to the decisions concerning discipline. Consequently, mercy versus judgment dilemma issues are a daily part of a principal's world. Many times as I sat in discipline hearings and determined whether a student was assigned to our discipline-based alternative educational placement unit, I heard parents and students ask for one more chance. In this equation were concerned parents who were sure that mercy was the right solution. On the other side, there was an assistant principal and teachers who were at their wit's end with the student, and they wanted justice. Both decisions would be right, and both decisions could be controversial. What will be my decision as a principal? How will I justify these decisions and maintain the courage to make the difficult decisions and stay the course?

Recently, as I interviewed educational leaders about resolving ethical dilemmas, the narratives provided valuable insight into the role of the principal and the complexities of decision making. The educators that were interviewed shared a strong belief that ethical dilemmas were an integral part of their role as principals, and that these decisions required time and soul-searching. Additionally, they shared their insights into the principles that shaped their decisions in these dilemmas—honesty, fairness, compassion, and responsibility. Finally, the interviews yielded rich narratives concerning remembered scenarios and insight into how leaders shaped and were shaped by these experiences.

During my doctoral experience, while my basic values have not changed, I recognize that I have been shaped by my experiences, and in turn I have extended the circle to include those on my campus as we engage in our primary mission—educating our students. In this process, it is vital that we take the time to make sure that all students are being treated with equity and justice. We must remember that so long as there are humans in the equation, ethical dilemmas will have to be resolved. As an educational leader, these decisions will demand a commitment to equity for all students and the moral purpose to maintain our convictions. Emerson (2004) challenged us in this regard by noting, "That which we persist in doing becomes easier; not that the nature of the thing itself is changed, but that our power to do is increased" (p. 4). Our task is to be a champion for children.

COURAGE TO STAY THE COURSE

Duffy (2003) wrote of "unwavering courage" and educational leaders who "face fear and do what has to be done in spite of it" (p. 5). To accomplish meaningful reform, educational leaders have to be fierce in their commitment to their moral purpose. This courage provided the momentum for principals to remain committed to the ethical course. Expanding on the notions of moral courage and physical courage, Kidder (2002) differentiated between the application of courage and moral courage when he noted that physical courage was only one facet of courage—the "willingness to face serious risk to life or limb instead of fleeing from difficult encounters" (p. 5).

In Kidder's (2002) views, moral courage was not simply about facing physical danger; instead, "it's about facing mental challenges that could harm one's reputation, emotional well-being, self-esteem or other characteristics" (p. 5). As educational leaders, we found that these challenges confronted our moral values and tested our moral courage. If we "pass the white light of moral courage through the prism of our understanding of values, it breaks out into a five-banded spectrum: the courage to be honest, to be fair, to be respectful, to be responsible and to be compassionate" (Kidder, 2002, p. 5).

To be an educational leader whose personal and professional mission is to "promote the success of all students by engaging our moral courage and displaying honesty, equity, respect, responsibility and compassion" (Kidder, 2002, p. 5) is surely a worthwhile undertaking. However in reality, it is many times a frustrating and thankless task. Kidder (2002) described the process as choosing the "hard right against the easy wrong" (p. 6). Why would anyone want to take on such a challenge? Sokolow (2002) suggested this was "fundamentally an expression of what we are at the core of our beings . . . [a force within] a divine spark that guides us as we live our own lives and lead others toward a brighter future" (p. 35). Whatever drives one to aspire to be a leader, it is most important that this person is also driven to be an ethical leader with courage and moral purpose.

REFLECTION

Leadership savvy and strategies could be quite disturbing and detrimental unless they were built on a strong foundation of ethics. Kidder (1996) made a chilling correlation between leadership without ethics as exemplified by Hitler, Mussolini, and Saddam Hussein. Further evidence of this essential link between ethics and leadership can be derived from reading English jurist John Fletcher Moulton (1924)—"Mere obedience to law does not measure the greatness of a nation. [Such obedience] can easily be obtained by a strong executive, and most easily of all from a timorous people" (p. 67). Synthesized in terms of leadership, Moulton's concept could read, "Mere strength of leadership does not measure the greatness of the leader. . . . The true test is the extent the individual can be trusted to follow self-imposed laws—ethics" (Kidder, 1996, pp. 66–67).

Adding ethics to educational leadership imparted a definitive twist to an already complex task. As I wrote this chapter, reread articles, and revisited moments in my practice, I reflected on the following question: How has my educational journey affected my interpretation and application of ethical leadership? Clearly, new constructs are reshaping my definition of ethicality and leadership as I revisited the places that I have mentally and emotionally traversed. While working to construct enhanced meanings and understanding of the educational leader role, I reflected on the person that I was and I know that I will never be that person again. I question the person that I am right now, and I realize that "the best starting point for such reflection is the unfinishedness of my human condition" (Freire, 1998, p. 66).

Debra Mahfouz Jordan is a junior high principal in the Vidor Independent School District in Vidor, Texas.

2

RESEARCH, REFLECTION, AND RELATIONSHIPS: DISCOVERING THE 3 RS OF TEACHER-LEADERS

Gary Clarke

The best-educated human being is the one who understands most about the life in which he is placed.

—Helen Keller[1]

"Why would you want to go there?"

The words from my principal were hanging between us. They had struck me like a punch to the face. As I sat with my two mentoring administrators, my mind was racing, as I tried to pull some kind of response together before the silence became too noticeable, when the counterpunch came from another unexpected source. "That's the last place in the world I would want to work," said my instructional supervisor. This second thunderclap had also found its mark. The crowning blow from my principal was almost redundant: "You might be ruining your future."

What had started as an exciting, well-thought-out career move was now quickly spinning its way down the drain of desperation. I had purposely waited for this private, informal meeting to announce that I had made my first application for a school administrative position. Six years of school,

---

1. Section quotes are from www.wisdomquotes.com/cat_education.html (retrieved July 23, 2004).

late nights studying, reading, researching, and soul-searching had preceded my application as assistant principal of instruction at our district's "alternative" school. Six years had been vanquished in six seconds.

The scene described above is part of my journey as a teacher who would seek to be a leader. How I responded is important, but more important is the story of the journey that all of us make in seeking to lead others.

WHERE I WAS

I'm an outsider. In education, most teachers and, certainly, almost all administrators go through traditional college classes full of theory, pedagogy, and curriculum. These are the foundation classes accompanied by method and materials classes, called M&Ms, that shape aspiring teachers' early training. However, the alternative teaching plan I had completed followed a practical, functional strategy of addressing the skills and strategies that could be applied in any classroom. Of course, I didn't know Horace Mann from John Dewey, but it never seemed to matter to my students.

My journey as a teacher always included a vision of leading as an administrator. With that goal in mind, I had actively pursued certification and training in principal preparation programs. Entering into education via alternative certification made me realize that I would have to overachieve in my preparation in order to compete with the more traditionally trained teachers. As an outsider, seeking the ultimate insider's job, I felt the need to work harder and to be better than the other teachers. That didn't mean that I upstaged them; it just meant that I had to excel and learn my craft. Also, coming from a nontraditional background into a very traditional profession meant that I had to pass every inspection. I couldn't afford to look or act too differently. That would only confirm that I really was an outsider. In short, I was looking for an edge to overcome the perception of being different. I found that edge in higher education.

Many teachers spend their summers and weeknights going to school to get advanced degrees and training. Most of these will obtain a master's degree that qualifies them for administrative or supervisory positions. Traditionally, this advanced training is focused on the duties and responsibilities that principals and supervisors are given to best manage schools. Upon completing this training, a teacher might begin to perform administrative duties on the campus by volunteering his or her extra time. I did this, but still felt like an outsider. There had to be a better way to reach my goals.

Before the ink was dry on my master's degree, I was thinking about getting my Ph.D. or Ed.D. An advanced degree that so few educators ever obtain would be the ultimate edge. No one could question my training or preparation. The doctoral degree would be the trump card played by the ultimate outsider.

WHERE I WAS GOING

Upon entering an educational leadership doctoral program, I realized that the stakes were higher. I was going to obtain an Ed.D. that would surpass the master's degrees (usually in education) that most principals and assistant principals had. I would be catching up with the traditionally educated teachers in a manner that would be respected—higher education. I simply viewed the process as one that would alter perceptions and misconceptions of my background by others, but what I found was a life-changing transformation.

The transformation process began with studies of leadership philosophies and theories. I began to understand that education is a battlefield of conflicting beliefs and values about schooling. I also understood that I would have to take a stand based on my own perception of these beliefs and values. This became a critical juncture in my life. The decisions I made would determine what was important to me in my daily practice as an educator. Further, these decisions would shape others' perception of me as a future administrator.

This process involved studying theories, philosophies, and practices as discussed by authors such as Dewey (1916), Duffy (2003), Foster (1994), Murphy (2002), and Starratt (1991) with an eye toward considering how different belief systems can influence student outcomes in classrooms. In short order, I realized that I believed that schools and school cultures can be positively changed by the same people who work in the schools right now, the teachers. Because I considered outcomes important and because I believed that people can control change, I knew that I was a pragmatist with a progressive view that in changing school cultures and outcomes, we impact our society as well.

My beliefs evolved quickly into an understanding that those changes had more potential for a lasting and positive impact if they occurred in the context of promoting democratic values. I also realized that those changes were more likely to occur in a caring, collaborative context that also sought equity and social justice within the school community. I strongly connected to the idea that all people had a stake in what happens in our schools and that their voices should be heard in the discourse about education.

THE 3 RS OF TEACHER-LEADERS

My belief that we could change education and, as a consequence, change our world had thus acquired a critical focus within the context of democratic values—values that our country has been pursuing and refining for 200-plus years. The acquisition of those beliefs is the story of an educator seeking to lead others: a teacher becoming a leader to lead teachers. This process would include how I came to understand that these concepts are linked together in a way that includes scholarly training, personal application, and, most importantly, understanding how other people must be included for change to occur. This process of research, reflection, and relationships is what I call the 3 Rs of teacher-leaders.

Research

> Man's mind, once stretched by a new idea, never regains its original dimensions.
>
> —Oliver Wendell Holmes Jr.

My scholarly training has been centered on concepts that John Dewey (1916) wrote about with passion. He proposed that we had to consider the consequences of not just *what* teachers taught but *how* they taught. He advocated that society must be responsible for considering how the future was to be shaped in a better way and that "the school is its chief agency for the accomplishment of this end" (p. 20). Moreover, his perseverance in pursuing these goals reflected his commitment to a noble cause.

In a very real sense, the conflict Dewey described is still timely and relevant. It remains contested, and, therefore, the future of education, and by extension, our society, is still in doubt. The struggle for democratic schools that reflect a caring leadership remains; the vigorous pursuit of those high ideals is a reasonable, respectable, and responsible goal for all aspiring teacher-leaders.

Many have influenced my journey in scholarship, but I am captivated by the vision of Starratt (1991) who pointed out that our schools must "serve a high moral purpose, to prepare the young to take their responsible place in and for the community" (p. 191). While it seems simplistic, his reference to future generations focuses on both context and purpose. By using "in and for" in conjunction with "responsible place" and "community," he implies the very definition of a democracy, that our voices are not only participatory but that all of us are responsible and should necessarily be motivated towards improving our collective experience.

Understanding that positive changes can occur in our schools leaves open the question of who might be responsible. While much research focuses on principals as leaders, none of that research excludes teachers from actively participating. My personal conclusion is that while we traditionally view principals as leading schools, that view places the teacher-student relationship in a subordinate context. Contextually, all positive changes imply significant changes in what happens with students, in each classroom, in every school. That context suggests that teachers are or must be leaders. Regardless of changes that principals plan and implement, teachers carry the banner forward to the objective. Teachers are leaders. The collaborative context is undeniable and unavoidable, becoming what Duffy (2003) calls the "great multiplier" as it spreads authority and influence throughout schools (p. 31).

As these thoughts and the supporting research continued to come together in my studies, I was aware that I was changing. My conversations with other teachers had begun to change. I was no longer complaining about moody assistant principals, unnecessary faculty meetings, or central office politics, I was talking about creating school leadership councils and wondering how to motivate teachers to come out of their classrooms and find their voices.

> Great minds discuss ideas, mediocre minds discuss events, small minds discuss personalities.
>
> —Eleanor Roosevelt

Reflection

> I hear and I forget. I see and I remember. I do and I understand.
>
> —Confucius

As my scholarship evolved, I became convinced that the best focus is not leaders changing their school cultures, but rather leaders changing their knowledge about themselves and their practice in the context of enabling democracy and caring in that culture. By questioning our motives and reasoning within our own practice, leaders can foster other leaders. Reflection enables our potential to critique and grow in our practice. Reflection enables us to free ourselves from the mistakes of our past. By enabling reflection in others we are enabling their potential for freedom as well.

I began to realize that by critically focusing on reflective and reflexive techniques as tools in shaping my practice, I was learning to enable myself to understand how educational policy informs, either positively or negatively, that practice. In the reflective process of scholarship, I could continuously break down and reconstruct my own knowledge within the construct of my personal practice. When I used a reflexive process to critique my practice within the context of my school, I was enabling myself and, ultimately, others to create cultures of their own choosing that reflected the values inherent in democratic, caring schools. It was in the "doing" of Confucius that I was learning, after reflection, what I needed to know as a leader. Duignan and Bhindi (1997) said it this way: "How can anyone presume to lead others forward towards 'a vision' if he/she is unsure of where he/she stands on important educational and moral issues" (p. 199). By situating my personal leadership within a cycle of scholarship, critique, and improvement, I was becoming a teacher-leader.

There remained a final part of my evolution to understand. How could a leader "teach" others the power of this leadership cycle that I was learning? More importantly, how did I break through to teachers who did not work in schools with principals willing to share authority and power? I could certainly see how I would do this as a principal at a school. Having studied leadership theorists, such as Duffy (2003), Donaldson (2001), Foster (1994), Fullan (2001), Murphy (2002), Sergiovanni (1992), and Starratt (1991), my research was growing toward an understanding of how to lead a school. The question was, how exactly could I engage others to believe in my vision? What would make them follow me? I was to keep asking and re-asking this question until I read a book by Margaret Wheatley (1999) that changed my life.

I have no special talents. I am only passionately curious.

—Albert Einstein

Relationships

To make a system stronger, we need to create stronger relationships.

—Margaret Wheatley (1999, p. 145)

In understanding the power of relationships, we need first to understand ourselves. If we consider the circumstances in our lives when we have been willing to pay any price, climb any obstacle, or go the extra mile, invariably it has been in the context of dedication or inspiration, often with others providing the inspiration or leadership that we followed. Equally important, we trusted those leaders to take us somewhere that both parties agreed was "better" than where we began. Duffy (2003) acknowledges how leaders can order people to change, but points out that their compliance results in minimum success and effort. What leaders really want is commitment, where followers "willingly and enthusiastically support change and perform" (p. 9). The missing component that motivates and enables their performance is trust.

All powerful relationships are based on trust and its resulting product, commitment. Trust implicitly resides in the eye of the beholder. Consider how trust is born of close scrutiny, a judgment based on our observation of an individual or process while he or she performs. Trust is derived from people watching us walk after hearing us talk. Trust is invariably spoken with our mouths and travels through our ears, but it is only proven through our eyes. By proving themselves in their follower's eyes, leaders are able to reach the hearts of those they would seek to lead.

When leaders arrive at the point of understanding that relationships are the key in leading others in schools, they become teacher-leaders, teaching others their own essence. By thus modeling the essence of our profession in our own practice, we become leaders who teach the hearts of other leaders to teach others' hearts as well. Teacher-leaders are then able to create others creating others. Joseph Murphy (2002) critically observed this as a leadership style evolving from a power construct of management into a relationship construct of trust and commitment: "They must learn to lead not from the apex of the organizational pyramid, but from a web of interpersonal relationships—with people rather than through them. They must learn to lead by empowering rather than by controlling others. There is as much heart as head in this style of leading" (p. 188). Ultimately, Murphy envisions that the very best leaders figure out a way to capture the hearts and minds of all members of their organization.

So, finally, I had arrived at a point of understanding that leaders must actively engage everyone in a vision of what positive changes could occur when a cycle of research, reflection, and relationships is enabled. Wheatley (1999) refined this further by urging all members to strive to "co-create their environment" (p. 46). By envisioning a democratic culture, nurturing trust and commitment, and enabling others to "co-create," I would become a successful principal. As their principal, my teachers would follow me as I taught them the cyclical power of the 3 Rs. I would break apart the old notions of management by sharing my authority and power with the teachers. We would co-create a new school with new visions and renewed hope.

Still, my questions continued to linger about teaching teachers this powerful leadership cycle. Would my perceived and real authority over them interfere with the delicate balance of shared power in our schools? What about all the other teachers who worked in schools where principals refused to share power? Was there a better place to teach teachers to become leaders? Was I maximizing the potential impact I could have as an educational leader by aspiring only to be a principal?

> Education is not the filling of a pail, but the lighting of a fire.
>
> —William Butler Yeats

WHERE I AM

This would normally be the perfect spot to include a description of a successful job search and my ensuing career as a successful principal. However, reality seldom cooperates with scripts and, instead, I must send the reader back to the beginning of the chapter for the description of my rather unsuccessful interview. That interview is but one small part of my journey in education.

Shortly after that episode, I began teaching college classes. Most of the classes had both experienced teachers and novices. As I began to talk about trust and commitment, democratic culture, caring, and co-creative power structures with my students, I saw lights come on and eyes open. I realized that the message was both real and potent. I also realized that because I was their teacher and not their principal, I posed little threat. They were free to explore new ideas; after all, that is what teaching and learning is about . . . exploring our limits and exceeding our expectations.

Suddenly, I had found a new opportunity, a new power to share. By becoming a teacher-leader, I had found a way to lead others in leading others. By enabling their voice within my classroom, I was setting in motion new expectations and new hopes. I was teaching the 3 Rs of teacher-leaders and together we were co-creating a new vision of schools. These were schools where teachers' voices are not silent, but rather engaged in fervent pursuit of democratic values and equity through caring, collaborative practices. By leading them to use the cycle of research, reflection, and relationships, I was giving voice to our collective vision of better schools and better lives. As I taught, I was leading them through teaching to become teacher-leaders. Almost as suddenly as my vision of becoming a principal was vanquished . . . I was redeemed. I had now become the ultimate insider—a teacher of teachers.

> Education either functions as an instrument which is used to facilitate integration of the younger generation into the logic of the present

system and bring about conformity or it becomes the practice of freedom, the means by which men and women deal critically and creatively with reality and discover how to participate in the transformation of their world.

—Paulo Freire

Gary Clarke is a special education teacher in Shreveport, Louisiana, and an adjunct university instructor at Stephen F. Austin State University in Nacogdoches, Texas, and Louisiana State University in Shreveport, Louisiana.

3

PRACTICE TO PASSION

Delinda Neal

> Sometimes the difference between being ordinary and extraordinary resides in the moment at which passion enters what we teach and how.
>
> —Author Unknown

FINDING MY SWING

I cannot remember the first time I held a golf club in my hand, or the first time I hit a golf ball and watched it sail through the air. I grew up in a home where playing golf was a part of family outings and, because I was the youngest of three children, I learned the game of golf by watching my parents and two brothers. None of them had ever received professional lessons but somehow they seemed to have good swings and they always had a lot of fun. For individuals who do not play the game, the golf swing is very technical and it takes much practice and professional help to be able to hit the shots necessary to be successful.

During my childhood I played the game on weekends with my family; in junior high, I finally beat my mother and to me this was like winning the U.S. Open. As far as I was concerned, I had reached my peak in this game.

When I was a freshman in high school, I became friends with a junior on the golf team who was extremely good and she encouraged me to join the team. That year I played on the team and quickly learned that I did not know enough about the game to be competitive. Since I am the type of person who hates to lose, I knew that I needed to raise the level of my game.

During the summer of my freshman year, I practiced tirelessly. I hit golf ball after golf ball trying to find the perfect swing. Most golfers remember the first time the golf club finally connects with the ball that results in the perfect shot. This memory occurred when I was fortunate enough to be on the same driving range with a man, Joe Bob Golden, who stopped practicing to watch a teenage girl whack a golf ball. This man was the father of one of the girls on the high school team. His daughter, Kate Golden, was at the time one of the best junior golfers in the country and today plays on the LPGA tour. The fact that he was watching me made my hands sweat, my muscles tense, and my heart race, resulting in several wayward shots.

Mr. Golden asked if I would like some help. I believe he recognized my nervousness and the feeling of inadequacies because he began to tell me the good things about my golf swing. He told me to put my club down, directed me to a bench, and began asking questions about my knowledge of the game. He explained the importance of the grip on the club, the stance of the feet, the swing plane, the power of timing, the impact, and the follow-through. He pointed out that I needed to apply the fundamental skills and make them work for me. He affirmed that I had the skills but putting the "why" with the "know-how" would help me find my own swing.

He then took me back to the driving range and what happened that day was something that I will never forget. Understanding why I was doing what I was doing helped me connect with the golf ball like never before. He also showed me ways to evaluate my own swing so that when bad shots were hit, I would understand how to fix it. That day he empowered me to be the coach of my own game. During that school year I practiced smart, watched golf tournaments on television, read golf magazines, and became obsessed about becoming a better player. During this process, I became a more confident and competitive golfer. Because I understood the concepts behind the game, that season, I found *my* swing.

The next school year, our team won the 4A state golf tournament and I was proud that I was able to contribute. During that tournament, I saw Mr. Golden as I was walking off of the eighteenth green. I was very excited because I had played great, and he was there to congratulate me on my round. He told me that he had followed my group for several holes and saw me make some good shots. He said he was happy to see that I had improved my skills and he noticed how much fun I had playing the game. That year, golf ceased being just a game for me. Golf became my passion.

ACQUIRED LEADERSHIP

As of today, I have been an educator for 15 years, 12 as a teacher and 3 as a campus administrator. I acquired my leadership skills in much the same way that I acquired my golf swing. As I was growing up, I watched my dad, who was a preacher, lead people in a church setting. I watched my mom influence hundreds of young girls' lives as a summer camp director. Leadership qualities were visible to me as a young child, and I believe that watching the two individuals who meant the most to me helped me assimilate the skills and beliefs to be successful as a teacher.

I had an additional role model enter my life during my eighth year as a teacher. This individual served as my principal and as I watched her lead a troubled campus into a professional learning community, I gathered the knowledge of leadership skills. I internalized the growing process and after I obtained a principal's certificate and started my first administrator's job as an assistant principal at a junior high, I sought to imitate this wonderful mentor and bring into my practice the experiences and knowledge that I had gained from her.

My second experience as a leader began when I accepted a job as an elementary principal at a low-performing campus. I knew that I would have to put into action all the skills that I had acquired from my mentors. The teachers on my campus needed to work together, the curriculum needed to be aligned, all students needed to believe in themselves, the building needed to be groomed, the staff needed to feel supported and praised, and the parents needed to become involved. In other words, major changes needed to take place and I needed to lead the charge.

I used the caring traits that I learned from my father to build relationships with my students, staff, and parents. I used the cheerleader qualities of my mother to encourage the hard work of the students. I imitated the process that I learned from my former principal—and the school blossomed into a wonderful place to learn. At this point I felt that I had reached a plateau in my career.

FINDING MY GAME

Just as I had an experience in my golf career that helped me excel, I also had a life-changing experience as I practiced in educational leadership. It all began when I applied and was accepted to an educational leadership doctoral program.

I entered the program confident that I could practice leadership because I had just finished a productive year. But throughout the first year of the program, I was exposed to theories and philosophies that explained the concepts behind leadership skills. It became clear to me the importance of building relationships through the readings of Duffy (2003) and Donaldson (2001). By being just and fair, I was following the works of Dewey (1916). Noddings (1999) and Barth (1990) encouraged my heart to keep caring for all children no matter what ethnicity, ability, or class.

Just as the golf teacher helped me connect with the golf ball, professors helped me connect my practice with theories and philosophies. By connecting the "why" with the "know-how," I experienced a change in myself that started an exploration for answers that would help me improve the educational situation not only for the students on my campus but also for all students in the state of Texas. I was guided through a self-evaluation process that helped me recognize the strengths and challenges in my practice. New learnings provided the spark that resulted in an inner fire in me to question policies and curriculums that are present in education today.

I know exactly when the spark ignited. It happened during the first summer in class. Our professor asked us to critically analyze a situation in our practice that we felt was unfair to children and present a solution that was well grounded in the literature. The topic that I wrote about that day was on statewide assessments. One of my specialties is the ability to raise test scores. In fact, the reason why I was hired at my current school was to raise the level of performance on the statewide tests. Yes, the school was successful—but looking back, the focus was centered on teaching the test, not the whole child. It was not uncommon for me to *stress* the importance of the test and remind the struggling child of the consequences of failing the test. Even staff members were uptight during nine-week exams because I was hovering outside their classrooms waiting for the results. Looking back, I fear that some of the tactics I used to raise the level of concern for students and staff most likely harmed the self-esteem of some children and left my staff wondering if I trusted their abilities. The most important test day of the year, children were physically ill from test anxiety; they cried during the test and staff members were overly stressed. I know I contributed to this because of my own stress and ambitions. Looking back I realize that I was playing the state's accountability game, not *my* game.

As I was writing the paper for my class, I remembered feeling somewhat emotional because I knew that I had participated in harmful discussions and fear tactics in regards to tests. Guilt came over me like a black cloud and I knew that I needed to make a change in my leadership practices. What resulted from this critical process was a more child-centered leader. And I made a vow that I would never participate in those harmful practices again.

I also realized during that year that I must expose children to much more than test-taking knowledge and skills. Dr. Robert Starratt, a professor at Boston University, spoke to our doctoral cohort in the fall of 2003. He emphasized that educational leaders must bridge high-stakes testing with authentic learning. He challenged us to present kids with opportunities that will help them look into their own lives, to examine the big picture, and to use the high standards as an excuse to make a difference in the future of the child. Using the teachings of Dr. Starratt, I began to understand the concepts of authentic leadership. The next step was to put the concepts into my practice. Just as with golf, I was learning to perfect my swing.

During the 2003–2004 school year, the students and staff that I led were not subjected to the pressure in regard to test results. Yes, we still prepared the kids for the exams and the expectations were high but instead of the stressful strategies, I praised them and encouraged their great efforts. This helped the students to believe in themselves, which made all the difference in their performance. It also provided them with a level of confidence during the actual test taking. When the results were published by the state, the students who were once labeled "low performing" achieved the highest level of accountability rating in Texas. This school year, my heart was full of pride and joy as I witnessed the growth in my students and staff. I had fun this year because I chose strategies that encouraged the heart of the child. This experience helped me find *my* swing in the game of accountability.

FUTURE

In the fall of 2003, my superintendent had told me that I would be opening a new elementary school the following year. I went through many challenging tasks, including a staff reassignment process, while trying to make sure my teachers and students remained focused on the task at hand. The fact that my leadership skills were affirmed by literature kept me confident while charting unknown territory.

This school year (2004–2005) I will have the opportunity to establish a culture that mirrors the teachings of my coaches. Being cognizant of my own values and beliefs and the realization that I do affect others around me has opened my eyes to a new responsibility as a leader.

If I am to make knowledgeable decisions, then I have the responsibility to become critical and not be satisfied with the status quo. I must observe the educational world around me with a critical lens in order to ensure equity and justice within the community that I serve. In order to be an authentic leader within my setting, I must uncover the distortions that exist in our language and our view of the world. I need to ask, "On whose behalf do I use my power?" (Quantz, Rogers, & Dantley, 1991, p. 97). I must allow all voices and arguments to be heard regardless of race, class, and gender. If I am truly committed to children, then I must critique the present order and I must believe that change is possible.

Lastly, if I am to truly be transformed into a scholar-practitioner leader, I must have the political and moral courage that works to empower followers to be leaders. I must not be afraid to speak against rules and regulations that will harm children and the community. The individuals I lead should see someone who genuinely cares about the human race, including the students and the parents of the students. My mind and heart have been opened to a "new scholarship" where "the practitioner as a scholar of practice, seeks to mediate professional practice and formal knowledge and theory through disciplined inquiry, and uses scholarly inquiry and practice to guide decisions on all levels of educational activity" (Jenlink, 2001, p. 7).

I have taken this knowledge and applied it to my leadership game. I intend to share with my staff and students this "new scholarship" through a series of learning experiences during the year. For example, I am in the process of creating a staff development series that emphasizes common vision, building relationships, and teaching for learning. Because the knowledge gained in the staff development will connect with our practice as educators, the experience will raise the level of learning not only for the staff but for our students as well.

CONNECTIONS

My experiences this year in education have been similar to the year I spent trying to find my golf swing. Through the teachings of a man who understood the game, I learned to connect the "why" with the "know-how" that helped me find *my* swing. When I finally found *my* golf swing and learned to connect with the golf ball, the game turned into a passion. Just as I learned from Mr. Golden, I applied the teachings of my readings and discussions from our doctoral classes. I discovered the theories and philosophies that support my leadership practices and I found that I cannot quench my thirst for more knowledge that will help me make a difference in young lives. I have connected practice with theory and I know this will guide me to encourage teachers to do the same. This journey of knowledge has changed my life personally and professionally. Leadership has ceased being just a practice for me; the quest for authentic leadership is now my passion.

Delinda Neal is principal at Thomas J. Rusk Elementary School in Nacogdoches, Texas.

4

ONE EDUCATOR'S JOURNEY: GETTING ON BOARD THE CHANGE TRAIN TOWARD A CULTURE OF SUCCESS

Stephen D. Patterson

It has been said that a fish would be the last creature on earth to discover water, so totally and continuously immersed in it is he. The same might be said of school people working within their culture.

—Roland Barth

INFLUENCES OF LEADERSHIP ON CAMPUS CULTURE

On a golf course one Saturday afternoon in the spring of 2001, I ran into a fellow educator who was an assistant principal from a nearby district. Recently, he had been named the principal at a middle school in a district across town. He asked if I was still working on my administrative certification. I explained that I was, but had not yet completed all of the coursework.

He encouraged me to apply for his old position. I told him that I would love to, but that I was not yet certified. He admitted that this could be a problem but that the interview experience would be valuable. I agreed with this logic and promised that I would apply on Monday.

The district with the vacancy was known for being a great place to work. Consequently, teaching and administrative positions rarely came open because, once employed there, people seldom left. Instantly, I was curious with the possibilities of potentially being employed in this organization.

Monday afternoon I stopped by the personnel office and submitted my resume and employment application. Within a few days, I received a phone call informing me of my interview time. The days leading up to that first interview were filled with anxiety. However, my interview with the building principal went well, and the following week, I interviewed with a teacher committee and was very hopeful about the possibility of being the new assistant principal. Although there was obviously some concern over my lack of certification, I felt that by the end of the year I could complete my coursework and successfully pass the certification exam.

Within a few days, I received a phone call from the district informing me that I had not received the job. The district felt that they needed a certified administrator to fill the position. Though I was upset, there were still many things I wanted to accomplish as a teacher. I knew that there would be other opportunities, but they were not likely with this district because of its popularity.

I became determined to finish my administrative degree and certification. Over the next year, I worked very hard at both. When the school year came to a close, I had completed a great year teaching math and I also had earned my administrative certificate. I began looking at district employment vacancies, hoping to find an assistant principal position at a local school.

DEFINITION OF CULTURE

Campus cultures have always been of interest to me, although during the early years of my teaching career, I had no idea what school culture really was. There is little doubt that culture is one of the two or three most complicated words in the English language (Williams, 1976). In fact, Berger (1995) estimated "that anthropologists have advanced more than a hundred definitions of culture" (p. 136). Generally though, the definition of organizational culture is "a pervasive way of life or set of norms" (Handy, 1993). It was apparent to me that rituals and traditions were prevalent in the school setting. Based on this, the definition of culture that I have come to use is "the way things are done in daily operations."

CULTURE CLASH

In my very first teaching position, my campus was led by a strong and effective principal whose word was final and unquestioned by staff and students. He always reflected genuine care for all and his ideas were sound and served the betterment of the campus. Teachers and students respected and admired his leadership. Consequently, I experienced being part of a productive staff that was very dependent upon the guidance of the leader. State standardized test scores rose to a level that was above average. Students seemed to enjoy coming to school. Parents and community were supportive. This building was a very good place to begin a career in education.

In my third year on this campus, a new superintendent was appointed. His leadership style was very autocratic. Within the fist month of his tenure, the sparks began to fly between my principal and him. A major cultural clash of the titans had begun. The staff on this campus was caught in a tremendous crossfire. The order and routines that were the culture of this campus had become disrupted. Culture allows for a set of norms that permit individuals to function within a system. This concept was confirmed by Nomura (1999) when he wrote, "Culture provides stability, fosters certainty, solidifies order and predictability, and creates meaning" (p. 19). When the culture of this school was altered, seemingly overnight, it was as though the foundation of the school had been shaken.

Faculty and staff morale suffered during this time of conflict. Bitterness and skepticism appeared to accompany most all central office memorandums. The culture of the school had become uneasy and individuals became guarded. By this time, my wife was employed in the same district on another campus. We opted for the life preservers before the proverbial ship sank and sought jobs in neighboring districts.

Today, when I reflect upon this incident, I am amazed by the power of one leader to influence the school culture. Leadership can build trust, relationships, and collaboration (Wheatley, 1999). However, leadership can also create a culture of skepticism, distrust, and rebellion. I did not see these truths so clearly years ago when this happened.

CONTINUED STRUGGLES

My next position was in a school with a very authoritarian leader. For example, he instructed that all supplies be kept under lock and key, and restricted access to information. Communication with staff was a two-hour faculty meeting every Wednesday. In this environment, teachers were told what to do and when to do it. I quickly learned that nonconformity, even if it was an improvement over the weekly directive, was likely to be punished with ridicule and documentation for insubordination. Students were treated with regimentation, second only to military boot camp.

Most teachers at this school did only enough to get by and students rebelled at the first sign of a lack of adult presence. The controlling nature of the leadership left staff and students unenthused and dehumanized. They were crying out for a culture of dignity and an opportunity to have decision-making power.

At this major crossroad in my life, I was presented with two opportunities to leave the education profession. My math background made me appealing to the stock brokerages that I contacted. The opportunity with these organizations would be very lucrative and fulfilling. My wife and I had two children under the age of three and we were beginning to struggle financially. Because I was so unhappy with the leadership at my school, my professional creativity was stifled and my professional growth was nonexistent. But, despite my unhappiness, I still believed that education was a calling, much like the ministry.

I knew that my contribution to the world was going to be made in the hallways of our nation's schools, not on the ticker tape of Wall Street no matter how appealing it seemed at the time. Ultimately, I decided to stay at this school, but I committed to begin graduate studies so that I could someday create the culture that I was longing for as a teacher. In graduate school, my professors began introducing me to the concepts of leadership and its influences on culture. Finally, I had a vocabulary to identify what it was I had been observing all of these years.

WHERE DO I BEGIN?

Even though my graduate classes were helpful, I still felt unprepared to adequately alter a toxic campus culture. Even though I now knew what culture was, I did not know what authors or journals to read for research on the subject, nor did I know other professionals whom I could engage in dialogue about how to change campus culture from negative to positive. Then I enrolled in a doctoral program in educational leadership. At this same time, I was appointed as assistant principal at a very successful high school in a nearby district.

Test scores were high, staff and students gave the appearance of being happy, and the community supported the school. This was the dream job I had been searching for in my career. The potential in this school was enormous. After I worked in this environment for only a few months, the untapped potential of this school culture was apparent. The culture of this campus was filled with wonderful possibilities.

IDENTIFYING A NEED FOR CHANGE

Along with another administrator, I soon discovered that we were dealing with a staff and student body that were satisfied with their present performance. The faculty performances were very good; however, there was little interest in continued professional growth and new initiatives. The teachers were successful in their practice and yet were wary of new initiatives and changes in practice. My fellow administrator and I were excited because the culture for the potential to evolve to new heights was immense, but so was teacher concern over the introduction of new methods and ideas.

Administrators did not want to be keepers of the status quo but leaders with purpose and vision. In order to alter culture, Nomura (1999) argued that educators must "understand your culture. You can't change what you don't know." (p. 19). Too often, the culture of the school has been ignored as numerous school reform panels have identified curriculum, pedagogy, and standardized tests as evidence of the need to change educational cultures. Culture building requires the will to transform the elements of school culture into forces that support rather than subvert the school's purposes. Of course, these acts violate the taboos of many school cultures, which is why culture changing is the most important, difficult, and perilous job of school-based reformers (Barth, 2002).

As new leaders to this campus, the other administrator and I knew that certain alterations to the school culture were necessary. Primarily, we needed to create a culture that supported risk taking and the acceptance of new ideas. Littrell and Peterson (2001) identified two important "characteristics of leaders [as] their abilities to both initiate and sustain action" (p. 316). To initiate successful action we knew we had to first understand the culture of our school. Who were the initiators and keepers of the school culture? Why had the culture evolved into what it was now? What forces sustained the culture of the school on its present course? Fullan (2002) wrote, "Thus, we needed leaders who can create a fundamental transformation in the learning cultures of schools and of the teaching profession itself" (p. 16). We wanted to be this kind of leader.

NURTURING CULTURAL CHANGE

During the first year of our tenure, the principal and I, as an administrative team, tried to make very few changes to prior practice. The few changes we did make were structural in nature, such as the master schedule, and relatively undisruptive to the lives of the teachers. We made few procedural changes. Our focus was on developing trust. By enhancing a culture of trust, we felt as though we could develop the relationships necessary to foundationally support change projects in the future.

The major initiative we took with teachers was done as an organizational learning project. All staff members attended a two-day training that focused on developing caring, positive relationships with students and one another. We witnessed some amazing growth within our teachers. The school culture was transformed before our eyes. The relationships teachers began to develop with one another and the students were immediately evident.

Prior to the start of the second school year with this faculty, the principal and I recognized more meaningful/deeper changes that were possible within the organizational structure. However, we felt that those changes needed to be developed by the faculty rather than ourselves. We also knew that meaningful changes should be done with established goals and vision statements (Hoyle, 2002).

Ultimately, the decision was made to take the entire faculty on an overnight staff development trip. Teachers were charter bused two hours away to an encampment. On the first evening, the teachers were shown a motivational PowerPoint presentation set to music that operated around the theme "Are You Ready?" The presentation presented pictures of staff and students from the previous year along with motivational messages and affirmations. This set the tone for the changes in philosophy and practice for faculty and staff on our campus.

The next step in the culture-building process was to identify where, collectively, our campus was. This presentation involved several movie clips from the Mel Gibson movie *We Were Soldiers*. The theme for the presentation was a commitment to one another and to our students that no one would be left behind. Data were shared with the faculty, which included failure rates, staff and student attendance percentages, state standardized test results, disciplinary referral numbers, and so forth. After concluding the presentation, several teachers were visibly emotional and almost all were actively engaged in discussion regarding the data they had just seen. Teachers were beginning to self-actualize the changes that needed to occur. I could hear veteran educators questioning their practice. Improvement ideas were being shared by members in small groups with one another. The change neurons in every brain in the room were firing like pistons in a locomotive. At that moment, we were a speeding change train that could not stop.

That evening faculty spent time by the campfire socializing. Teachers began to really get to know one another. Coaches sat with band directors and discussed hobbies. English teachers sat with math teachers discussing family. True relationships and understandings began to form.

The next day, teachers were divided into three groups. While two groups performed team-building activities outside, one group worked on one of three activities. The groups systematically rotated over the course of the day. Based on the data presented the previous evening,

GETTING ON BOARD THE CHANGE TRAIN

faculty wrote campus goals, a campus vision statement, and a faculty social contract. At the end of the day, the end product was an assimilation of what the three groups had communicated. In just under 36 hours, an environment had been created that produced the initiative and the plan for systemic cultural change. While administrators had obviously participated on a foundational level, teacher response was the catalytic driving force for what was created. It was truly beautiful.

SUSTAINING CULTURAL CHANGE

Currently, I produce a newsletter to the staff every four to six weeks reporting our current progress on the campus goals. Atop each newsletter is the campus vision statement so that we are constantly reminded of what we say we want to become. The letter includes affirmations of positive acts that have occurred and reminders of issues that are not aligned with the vision. This has been well received.

The Site-Based Decision-Making Committee meets once a month. This group has been empowered to make structural decisions and has the ability to address organizational learning needs. In this way, teachers are empowered through democratic practices. Department heads have been given much of the same latitude with regard to department-level decisions.

The culture of our school has become one of trust and love. The faculty of this campus has become closer than I could have ever believed possible. Because they have a true respect for one another, I see a transfer of that emotion to the students that ultimately will build a better environment for learning.

Across our nation today there is a tremendous emphasis on standardized testing; the concept of school culture is often last on administrative agendas. However, Barth (2002) challenges this emphasis by stating, "Show me a school where instructional leaders constantly examine the school's culture and work to transform it into one hospitable to sustained human learning, and I'll show you students who do just fine on those standardized tests" (p. 11). As our culture became more positive, our already high scores rose higher.

CONCLUSION

On a Saturday in the spring of 2002, as luck would have it, one day I encountered my friend from the golf course. We had not seen each other since the summer before. We talked about his first year as a campus principal and all that he had learned. He was enthusiastic about his experience and encouraged me to begin applying for jobs again.

I explained that I had finished my coursework and was now certified. I did not know of any job openings, but I was actively looking. He told me that the assistant principal position that I had applied for the previous year where I had been turned down because of my lack of certification had become open again, as well as the principal's position. I was amazed to hear this news. Once again, the position I had my sights originally set on was available. I applied and this time I was hired as assistant principal. At the same time, my friend was hired as the principal of the school.

This paper is about an administrative team creating a culture of success. My friend is part of that team, and I am the other team member. We are currently both doctoral students at two Texas universities. Every day, we come to school, we get on board the change train, and we continue toward creating, nurturing, and sustaining a culture of success.

Stephen D. Patterson is a high school assistant principal in Orange, Texas.

5

FROM TEACHING TO REACHING: CARING AS AN INSTRUCTIONAL IMPERATIVE

Jeffrey R. Schultz

> Those who help us center our work in a deeper purpose are leaders we cherish, and to whom we return love, gift for gift.
>
> —M. J. Wheatley (1999, p. 133)

I am a musician. I have been performing music for audiences large and small for nearly as long as I can remember. My earliest experiences as a musical performer were in my church, singing in the children's choir, either collectively or as a soloist. Elementary school afforded broader musical opportunities in the form of piano lessons, districtwide select chorus, musicals, and beginning band. Middle and high school provided further musical outlets with outstanding choral and wind ensembles as well as performance opportunities in the all-state band and choir. When it came time to choose a career and enter college, there was no question that I would pursue a future in music.

When I entered college, my musical achievement and performance continued to blossom as I eagerly chased abounding opportunities within the collegiate musical realm. Because my solo recitals were consistently well attended, I found that I truly thrived on and thoroughly enjoyed the act of sharing music with others. My instrumental performing skills provided opportunities to solo with the wind ensemble, and the choral director constantly sought my singing skills. More opportunities and achievement awaited in graduate school where I found myself performing in orchestras, chamber ensembles, and wind bands, and as a soloist. For an artist, all of this performing, and the accolades that often accompany performance, can do a lot to create, feed, and stroke the artistic ego. I share my artistic development with you, not to toot my own horn (no pun intended), but to provide some background into my mindset as I entered my first teaching job out of college: It was all about me.

MISSED OPPORTUNITIES

At the age of 23 I began my first teaching job in a large Texas high school band program. I chose to work in Texas given that their band programs have a strong and widespread tradition of excellence in preparing students to become fine young instrumentalists. The band program in which I worked contained nearly 250 students participating in four different bands; I was hired as the second assistant director with specific responsibility to conduct the third and fourth bands. During the fall semester, the third and fourth bands were combined into one ensemble of approximately 120 students. Naturally, students are placed in bands by audition and ranked by ability level; therefore, I was conducting students of less advanced, and often marginal, musical knowledge and skills within a mass ensemble setting.

I vividly remember the first day of school and my preparation leading up to the first ensemble rehearsal. The music we played consisted of music for our marching band halftime show as well as music to accompany the drill team and to rally the fans in the football stands (Friday night football is also big in Texas!). As I greeted the students coming through the door, I remember feeling nervous, but also anxious to begin our music making; the students, of course, were also curious and anxious about their new band teacher. Granted, we had met one another during our last week of summer band practice, but I still did not know these students well enough to assess their playing skills and personalities. I had observed the top two bands' rehearsals earlier on that first school day and remember feeling confident about what musical elements to work on and how to run our first rehearsal.

Once the students had unpacked their instruments and found their assigned seats, we were ready to begin. Our rehearsal began with the B-flat scale, some tuning notes across the band, and a tuning chorale, and then it was time to touch on the music. I provided the downbeat and the introduction to our march sounded quite nice for the first of the year. But upon entering the first strain, things quickly fell apart. There was absolutely no semblance of musical line or any rhythmic integrity across the ensemble. What was a director to do? Stop, of course; simple enough. I would simply correct the problem(s) and get right back to it. I circled my arms and brought the ensemble to a stumbling halt.

To my dismay, a 120-headed monster began to rear its ugly heads. A cacophony of voices arose from gaping mouths and, suddenly, I could not even hear myself ask for the flutes, clarinets, and trumpets to play their line beginning at measure 9. So I did what I remembered my schoolteachers doing when disruptions would occur; I raised my voice above them all and yelled at them to BE QUIET! This cycle continued until the end of the hour: Play, stop, ask, yell; play, stop, ask, yell. Not an atmosphere worthy of learning, much less music making. I left rehearsal defeated and, frankly, insulted by the notion that some of these students would dare disrupt my music-making experience. You see, musical performance, until now, had been all about me.

I consulted with my colleagues about classroom discipline in a setting such as this. Their advice was appropriate and seemed logical. They explained that I must set the tone early in the rehearsal and if students were talking or otherwise disruptive, I must call them on it immediately so that other students knew that I meant business. So on day two I began rehearsal armed and ready. Again I greeted students at the door, and once they were settled into their seats, we began our warm-up routine. Upon the first directed stop for instruction, the uproarious cacophony began again and I spotted a flutist directly in front of me talking to her stand partner. I quickly addressed the young lady quite sternly, almost aggressively, yet I asked her politely to please not talk when we were stopped and I was instructing. Fair enough, I thought, but I was shocked when she spoke back to me in a slightly sassy tone saying, "I wasn't the only one talking" or something of that regard. She was most likely correct, but my pride and arrogance would never have allowed me to admit such a thing to her or anyone in the ensemble. I shot back a terse, frank retort and returned to rehearsal. Thankfully, the ensemble was quiet for a time, not necessarily because I had set the tone, but likely out of shock that I could be so direct and, perhaps, angry toward their fellow student.

The long and short of this tale is that discipline problems continued to plague my ensemble instruction throughout my first year of teaching, if not through my second. To make matters worse, by the second day of class I had ruined any possibility of building a positive relationship with this particular flute student and we continued to go head-to-head many times throughout her three years of appointment to my ensemble. These interactions were often verbally abrasive and demeaning for both of us. Subsequent disciplinary meetings with this student and my colleagues, administrators, and her parents did not bring an end to her behavioral disruptions. It is also safe to say that I became hypersensitive to this student's behavior and would quickly jump on any opportunity to point out her disciplinary shortcomings.

Reflecting upon this experience more than a decade later in a doctoral program, I realized how far off the mark I had been. Although it is entirely true that this student repeatedly misbehaved in my classroom, I have often wondered if I had demonstrated the smallest amount of caring towards her whether her behavior and participatory learning would have been different. There is no way that I can now know why she chose to behave the way she did. I do know that there is really no excuse for the way that I chose to behave in those circumstances unless I count my own inexperience and lack of a thirst for knowledge. Margaret Wheatley (1999) bestowed a possible explanation for the unfortunate learning experience that I may have provided for this student. She stated that in certain organizations

> leaders attempt to force better results through coercion and competition; sometimes they exhibit a flagrant disregard for people and their abilities. In such organizations, a high level of energy is also created, but it's entirely negative. Power becomes a problem, not a capacity. People use their creativity to work *against* these leaders, or in spite of them; they refuse to contribute positively to the organization. (p. 40)

There is no question that I was trying to coerce this young lady into my ideal of appropriate ensemble behavior. I also used competition by dutifully rewarding the good behavior of other students in hopes that other band members would help to police the ensemble through peer pressure. The result was exactly as Wheatley reported; this young lady used all of her creative energy to work against my leadership and continually refused to contribute positively to the organization.

AWARENESS

I recall that during my first teaching position, while passing through the halls, I would often be mistakenly asked for a hall pass. Here I was, six years out of high school, having earned a master's degree, still being confused for a high school student. In order to compensate for these misunderstandings (damn this baby face!), I worked hard to elevate my outward appearance through my use of language and in my professional demeanor. At some point I determined that placing distance between my students and myself would be a necessary step toward earning the respect that I felt I deserved, both from my students and colleagues. Here again, it was all about me.

Things did improve from a disciplinary standpoint over the weeks and successive school terms, and my ensembles made noted improvement during the tenure of my first teaching position. My next public school band job found me in the role as first assistant director. Working with an ensemble that contained students of higher ability level, combined with my own maturity, likely contributed to greatly reduced problems with discipline in this second teaching position. However, while I would say that this band experience was successful, I still found that I was having trouble reaching many of my students. Please don't get me wrong. During these early years of teaching, my students and I enjoyed some wonderful musical and shared personal moments together; however, deep down I always knew we were capable of greater things.

After just two years in my second teaching position, I accepted a position as assistant director of bands and instrumental instructor with a midwestern university. University music instruction had been my goal since undergraduate school and this would be my chance to show the world how much I had to offer. A large part of my responsibilities in this new position included the direction, both musical and organizational, of the college marching band. My students and I had, what I consider to be, a great season of performances (though the football team did not), and I ended the fall term feeling very proud of the improvements I had wrought in this college band program.

My other instructional responsibilities included private lessons for music education majors on their chosen instrument. This type of teaching is something that I deeply enjoy and is an area in which I have excelled. What I like so much about this type of instruction is that once I get beyond the fundamentals of tone production and technique, I get to work directly with the young musician's expressive capabilities. This requires a great deal of trust between a student and teacher because we begin to touch what is essentially their musical soul. Teaching of this type also requires that I, as the teacher, continue to practice, perform, and otherwise challenge myself to grow musically on a daily basis. Consequently, in addition to the large amount of time spent on marching and concert band preparation, rehearsals, and performances, I needed to make time to practice my own instrument and musicianship for a minimum of two hours per day.

While I considered that in this position I was a very giving teacher of time, energy, and heart within the instructional setting, I truly desired and guarded time alone for musical practice and preparation. So when a student would knock on my door in the middle of my score study or instrumental practice, I would literally roll my eyes, heave a deep sigh, and wonder what "they" possibly needed now. This type of behavior alludes to how I was most often impatient and unwilling to share of myself outside of the instructional environment. Still, I maintained that much musical and organizational progress had been made within my individual and ensemble musical settings. That is until I received my student evaluations at the beginning of the next term. Overall, they were quite positive but there was one that spoke bluntly to me about the way that I was treating students. In the space allotted for students to provide their own comments, one stated simply: "Needs to remove pole from butt." While at first, I had a good laugh about this comment, in retrospect (and this is the type of comment that never leaves one's psyche) this student could not have evaluated my educational demeanor more concisely.

This testimony prompted me to evaluate my actions and behaviors, not only in the instructional setting but outside of it as well. Was I really stuck up? Could this be what was preventing me from reaching some students? If so, where was I falling short? I began to carefully observe my colleagues within the music department who demonstrably had positive educational relationships with their students. What were these colleagues doing that I was not? How did they achieve respect as teachers and yet still develop close one-on-one relationships with their students? It was difficult to be so introspective, yet still the solution eluded me. There was no question, however, that during my years in this position I consciously attempted to open up to my students. As I did so, I noticed the elevated walls of respect, which I had worked so hard to build in my early years of teaching, slowly begin to crumble. All of this personal reflection led to a moment of clarity.

More than two decades of focusing on my own musical, educational, and artistic development had turned me into a conceited artist, one who craved acknowledgement, accolades, and respect in all of my musical doings in order to supplement my ever-growing artistic ego. Suddenly, I came to the realization that perhaps this incomplete feeling, this emptiness, in my teaching stemmed from the fact that I had distanced myself too far from the reason I chose a career in education in the first place: to share with others my love for and knowledge of music. Freire (1998) spoke concisely of this educational dilemma, asking, "How can I be an educator if I do not develop in myself a caring and loving attitude toward the student, which is indispensable on the part of one who is committed to teaching and to the education process itself" (p. 65).

Having now been in education for 10 years I believe that my commitment to the profession was always there; however, my commitment to the students had yet to develop. I arrived at the conclusion that teaching was not supposed to be about me—a difficult conclusion for a young teacher who spent more than half of his life aglow in the spotlight. Clearly, it was time for me to exit the stage and allow my students their opportunity to bask in the radiance of their own musical development, front and center. I needed to become fully available to the numerous needs of my students. At least by this point I had become aware of this greater pedagogical dilemma and could begin working toward open and giving relationships with my students.

FORWARD MARCH

Three years into my next collegiate teaching position found me entering a doctoral program in educational leadership. During my time in this program I have found the words, knowledge, and concepts that address how to cope with my artistic ego in an educational environment. For me, progress towards relinquishing the limelight and availing my true self to students and colleagues has come slowly, but steadily, and I have seen tremendous educational outcomes as a result. Wheatley (1999) insisted that within organizations "we need to become savvy about how to foster relationships, how to nurture growth and development" (p. 39). If only someone had shared this uncomplicated thought with me sooner! The act of educating, from my perspective now, is all about the building of relationships. Moreover, it is simply not possible to build relationships with students within the classroom environment only. Additionally, it is through these relationships, which invoke trust and caring between two individuals, that it becomes possible to be nurturing or nurtured whether you are the educator or the educated.

If only I could turn back the clock and work to foster relationships with some of the students that I have ignored, lost my temper with, or failed to reach in general, and try a little tenderness as a disciplinary or educational tactic. I now realize that I came to know so little about these students because I was not open to sharing myself with them. When working with such large groups as concert or marching bands, I have had the potential to relationally influence so many students in so many ways. My private instruction of future music educators now provides the opportunity to demonstrate that caring about students is imperative to the educational process.

Despite the students that I may have failed to reach in my early teaching, in the past few years I have heard from a number of former students via e-mail or rare person-to-person contact. Many have shared remembrances of our educational experiences together, and it is clear that I have touched these students positively and created a real sense of accomplishment and reward for their efforts. Contact with such numbers of students in an educational setting, unified in the purpose of shared musical learning and accomplishment, allows for the opportunity to develop a true sense of community. Jordan (1999) addressed this ideal of community within a musical ensemble. He maintained:

> The relationship between music teacher and classroom is a community. . . . But that relationship is much more than a simple interaction or acknowledgement of existence. It must be a union, a bond, a connectedness that brings human beings so close spiritually that they almost become one—equals on the same playing field. (p. 75)

This speaks directly to the issues that I began, and continue, to address. I toiled so hard for so long to separate and elevate myself from my students that there was never a chance for us to become a community, much less equals within the learning environment. Happily, I now begin each day with the knowledge that I must continue to tear down the walls to my educational and musical soul, fastidiously constructed with the mortar of my artistic ego, so that I can begin to reach more students as I enable them to more truly relate to me.

CODA

In my current position I no longer conduct large musical ensembles but instead teach primarily in a one-on-one environment. I have made progress toward my goal of availing myself to my students, and this simple act of caring has had a direct impact on student learning. A recent student evaluation (that also will also forever remain in my psyche) stated, "Mr. Schultz is the shizzle fa' sho!" I have ascertained the meaning of this language, and loosely translated it is equivalent to "Mr. Schultz is, most certainly, top-notch!" While I have miles to go yet, improvement can be noted in the way that members of my studio are brought together as a small community. It is my hope that the future of my teaching will be marked by this community ideal in addition to the standards of musical excellence that I persistently demand from my students. I continually remind myself that a knock on the door means that I have another chance to interact caringly with a member of this musical community. The more we care for one another within our musical groups, the stronger the bonds that connect our community will be. Imperatively, the person who sets the standard for caring within our community must be no one else but me.

In his book, *The Musician's Soul*, James Jordan (1999) cites his mentor Elaine Brown from an alumni lecture that she gave in 1988. She remarked, "We need to do a very simple thing. *And that is to care more.* It is so simple that it is elusive. Not a saccharine caring, but a deep down caring that is part of commitment. It is the same care that makes you commit to the human race and to yourself" (pp. 80–81). These words speak the true essence of why I teach: I teach music because I care to share knowledge; I teach music because I care to continue learning; I teach music to future educators because I care to share my hope for the future, one that is imbued with caring teachers, students, and communities. Thankfully I have come to see that teaching is not about me; it is about the students. Therefore, the most important reason that I choose to teach must be to reach students.

Jeffrey R. Schultz is currently the professor of tuba, euphonium, and music theory at Stephen F. Austin State University in Nacogdoches, Texas.

6

MAKING EDUCATION COUNT

Linda Bass

> Systemic redesign requires change-leaders who possess unwavering courage to do the right thing, a burning passion to educate all children, and a grand vision of what schooling can become for children, teachers, and communities.
>
> —Frank Duffy (2003, p. 4)

I stood in absolute disbelief as one of my top seniors told me that he really didn't know his plans after graduating from high school. It was graduation night, and as school principal, I was mingling with many of the seniors and their families during a reception. I suddenly realized that I was not the great principal that everyone thought I was. After all, isn't it important for graduating seniors to have some idea of what they are doing after high school? Isn't part of my responsibility as an educational leader to prepare students for success beyond high school? That night, my job took on a whole new dimension as I realized that some major changes had to occur in the way we prepared our students for postsecondary success.

During my next doctoral class meeting, our educational leadership cohort discussed the importance of being an authentic leader who truly cares for all students. My mind flashed back to graduation, and I began to connect the responsibilities that I had often felt students must shoulder with my responsibility to provide career awareness, education, and preparation for each student in my school. Until now, I had wanted the students to make good grades and wise choices, and to become successful in their own way. I thought of the many students who had graduated from my school that had not had the career education that they needed. I was beginning to realize that my commitment as principal had to be more passionate and caring regarding career preparation for each student.

ABOUT OUR SCHOOL

Our school was a great school in many areas, but not what it should be in career education, preparation, and awareness. Our football team enjoyed national acclaim. The coaches had worked hard for years to build a team that succeeded year after year. Our other sports programs were good, but faculty and administration agreed the girls' sports programs could be improved. Our drama program had been outstanding for years. I believe its success is due, even today, to the expertise of one teacher with passion and purpose in this area. The visual arts at our school were "off the charts" because one teacher fostered a love and appreciation for this program, which obviously bled over into her students.

The academic aspect of the school was getting better every year. For example, 3 years ago, we won third place in the regional literary rally (an academic competition) for several years. I felt that our school could win first place if we worked diligently to prepare the students for the competition. I called a meeting of the faculty and students who would be working together and challenged them to work even harder to convince others that our school was academically as strong as we knew it was. Not only did we win first place that year, but we won first place last year too.

To add validity to the claim that our school is improving every year academically, our high-stakes test scores continue to rise. Last year, for the first time, our chemistry and physics students entered a competition with some of the best schools in our area. We were the only rookies. When our students arrived, each group was given a paper bag with some supplies in it. In one particular situation, they were told to build a robot that worked three times, and they would be in the final competition. Our rookies won first place. I attribute that success in part to one teacher who eats, lives, and breathes science. Her group of students won three of the five competitions that day. Winning outside one's school due to raw talent and a solid educational background soon changes the reputation of the school. Our school reputation was growing, but I was still concerned about a huge part of each student's educational experience—career preparation. We had grown in so many ways; now it was time to work in this area.

IDENTIFYING MY PASSION

I was like a sponge soaking up information to share with my teachers and students about career preparation. One of our professors shared that my dissertation needed to be something about which I have a passion. That stuck in my mind. I realized that ensuring that all students have at least an idea of whether they are going from high school to work, to vocational school, to a community college, or a four-year college was my passion.

A cohort member told me about a school nearby that had revamped its program structure into career academies. Essentially, each high school student takes the required Carnegie units to graduate from high school, and electives are directly linked to individual postsecondary career aspirations. There were many questions whirling in my head about this new approach to education. During our next weekly faculty meeting, I explained what I had learned about career academies to my fellow administrators at my school. They were interested in learning more about career academies. A few days later, I contacted the school using career academies to see if our administrators could visit the school. The principal was delighted for us to spend the day with his administrators, teachers, and students to learn how they structured their program of instruction. Little did I know it, but this was a pivotal point in my career.

As the assistant principal of this school gave our administrators the grand tour, I realized that my leadership abilities had taken on a new dimension. During the past three years I had worked extremely hard with a group of wonderful students, teachers, and administrators to change the perception of our school from a "football factory" to an excellent school in the academics, arts, and athletics. It had been hard work and dedication to a calling to accomplish this worthwhile task. But this was different. I was now the pioneer of an innovative, beneficial program for my school. Thinking "out of the box" was not an easy thing for me. I had previously been a "project" principal. That is, I made a list of the things that needed to be accomplished at my school, included as many stakeholders as possible in their implementation, and completed many of these projects. But I was not leading my school in the right direction.

ACCEPTING A NEW CHALLENGE

Fullan (2001) identified the importance of mobilizing people to tackle tough problems because "leadership is not mobilizing others to solve problems we already know how to solve, but to help them confront problems that have never yet been successfully addressed" (p. 3). There is nothing wrong with being a project principal as long as the principal is cognizant of how leadership is used. Thus, knowing that my school was no different from the other good schools in our area, I knew that it needed something to make it more appealing.

My career now took another paradigm shift. I had never thought this deeply before about successful educational practices—until I began to apply some of the principles that I was learning in my ongoing studies. Furthermore, I had never had the civic courage to be an effective transformational leader. Duffy (2003) discussed the tremendous courage, passion, and vision that it takes to lead systemic change. He emphasized that "systemic redesign requires change-leaders who possess unwavering courage to do the right thing, a burning passion to educate all children, and a grant vision of what schooling can become for children, teachers, and communities" (p. 4). Also imperative to successful systemic change is to remember that leadership must be rooted in a culture of trust, commitment, and collaboration. What I was learning was changing my career and helping my school to improve in many ways.

Many meetings with our students, teachers, parents, and school board members provided valuable input into making career academies work for our particular school. Stakeholders began to take ownership of something that they had helped to create. This gave me a valuable opportunity to demonstrate my belief in our school community. Quite honestly, this was a giant step for me—to begin the discussion of something this important to our school and to all stakeholders. While I did not want to be caught in an unpleasant meeting, I realized that input from many people in the school family was important. Duffy (2003) boosted my confidence when he wrote, "It takes a courageous, passionate, and visionary leader to allow collaboration to happen because when you increase opportunities for genuine collaboration, you decrease centralized authority and power" (p. 10). Harris (2004) pointed out the importance of leaders empowering others in the school community and emphasized that empowerment happens "when leaders are willing to trust the wisdom and experience of others, when leadership is recognized and developed at every level" (p. 12). It is one thing to read these quotes in a doctoral program; it is quite another thing to be living in the middle of them!

Obviously, I knew there would be challenges to overcome in transitioning our school from its present curricula to career academies, but I also remembered Fullan's (2001) admonition that "effective leaders make people feel that even the most difficult problems can be tackled productively" (p. 7). It was important for me to maintain a sense of optimism and an attitude of never giving up in the pursuit of highly valued goals for our school. My enthusiasm that career academies could improve each student's preparation for life and my confidence in our school's faculty and staff soon became contagious throughout the school. I was reminded of Donaldson's (2001) idea of "active caring in which leaders are willing to accept the school's challenges and our current working conditions and relations and, despite the odds, to act on them" (p. 144). This was happening in our school, and it was helping the school to be a focused team.

CHAPTER 6

IMPLEMENTING A NEW CHALLENGE

Toward the end of the school year, a planning retreat for the next year's calendar, mission statement, vision, Southern Association of Colleges and Schools (SACS) accreditation, budget, staffing, professional development, and curriculum development was held. All administrators were asked to do a presentation for their area of responsibility. I knew that I wanted to do "the usual" presentation that a principal should do at this time, but would I dare have the courage to suggest a tremendous change in the way we educated and prepared our school's students and the important role of all stakeholders? I worked on my PowerPoint presentation for weeks making certain that I had included everything necessary for my colleagues to understand career academies and the changes that would need to occur in our present system. My presentation was research based, filled with the best practices, and contained pertinent information about the change process needed for our school. Although the other administrators of our school had visited the nearby school and were impressed with the school's career academies, I was not sure they understood the possibilities of making this work for our school. But it was important information to be shared; as Fullan (2001) had suggested, "the key to developing leadership is to develop knowledge and share it; if it is not mutually shared, it won't be adequately developed in the first place" (p. 132). Sharing the knowledge was not enough, however. It was still important that all stakeholders understood the career academy approach to education. Throughout the next few meetings at the end of the school year, I made several presentations that enabled our administrators, faculty, and staff to feel comfortable and confident about our new educational process of career academies.

Celebrating is an important part of making school an exciting and pleasurable place to be. According to Kouzes and Posner (2003), "Celebrations infuse life with passion and purpose. They summon the human spirit" (p. 113). Since we had included members from each stakeholder group in the formulation of our new approach to preparing our students for successful futures, we wanted to include everyone in the celebration time. Our students, parents, teachers, and administrators held an assembly to officially announce that our school would begin a pilot program with the seven career academies the next school year. They discussed how each academy would individualize the education and preparation of each student for postsecondary success, and explained that each student would have a faculty adviser with a passion for that particular career. There was also a time for questions and answers. What an exciting way to end the year! We realized that in the fall students at our school would not only be taking the courses required for a state diploma, but they would also be using their electives to pursue a career in something that accentuated their strengths and interests.

Throughout the summer our counselors and selected teachers helped to match students and mentors. This was such an exciting time in the school! We were actually seeing the dreams that we had for our students coming to life. Many of our seniors were attending classes to complete their Carnegie unit requirements, and then they were paired with professionals in their chosen career field. We had students shadowing doctors, physician assistants, veterinarians, lawyers, teachers, heating and air-conditioning experts, and dental assistants. Prior to career academies, these same students would have simply had part of their school day free because they had taken all of their required courses. Now, they were building a foundation for success in their postsecondary lives. Some students will probably find that this is not what they want to do with their lives. Others will realize that this is what they need to be doing. Still others will need to look further to see what career they are genuinely interested in pursuing. However, our main objective is being met daily. Students are looking at alternatives, trying them out, narrowing them down, and saving time, money, and energy before they graduate from high school. I wonder how many college seniors wish they had had this opportunity in high school.

Excitement is in the air at our school this year. The focus seems right. Administrators, teachers, staff, students, parents, and the community have a fresh vision that makes us feel good about where our students are headed with their dreams and aspirations. It is so exciting to see our students, their parents, and faculty advisers working together to assist each student in seventh through twelfth grades about their careers. Monthly meetings are scheduled, during which faculty advisers instruct students in a specific career about how to complete a resume, portfolio, interview, and internship. The most important aspect of this whole approach for me as principal is that a message is being sent to all stakeholders that every student has strengths and interests and is a vital part of society. Not all students are meant to attend college. Some are going from school to work, others are going to a vocational/technical school, and still others are going to college. But all students are important, and it is my responsibility as instructional leader of my school to ensure that each student is prepared, not only to do well academically but also to make wise choices regarding a career. This has become a passion for me. I truly believe it is the culminating activity of school—to prepare young people for postsecondary success.

Having been an elementary, middle, high school, and college teacher as well as a middle and high school principal for many years has been a rewarding calling in my life. However, not until I continued my education through a doctoral program did I fully understand "that instructional leadership, when it is done well, is transformational leadership" (Fullan, 2001, p. 62). In fact, I honestly never thought about being a transformational leader until then. I want my life to count for something even more than being a transformative leader. I agree with Fullan (2001) who said, "I want people to be able to say what I did was substantial. That it counted" (p. 62). When young people make good decisions about their lives and future careers because of the education and preparation at our school, I know that my life has counted.

Linda Bass is currently an administrator at Evangel Christian Academy in Shreveport, Louisiana.

SUCCESSFUL OR SIGNIFICANT? THE ROLE OF EDUCATIONAL GRACE

Jim Vaszauskas

> We were once made secure by things visible, by structures we could see. Now it is time to embrace the invisible.
>
> —Margaret J. Wheatley (1999, p. 58)

Harold Abrahams was a British Olympian who competed in both the 1920 and the 1924 Olympics and won gold and silver medals in track and field. He was arguably one of the greatest runners in Great Britain's history. In an important scene from the movie *Chariots of Fire*, Abrahams is dismayed because of a particularly bad performance and insists, "If I can't win, I won't run." His future wife counters this by saying, "If you don't run, you can't win."

This conversation relates the distinction between being successful and being significant. Harold Abrahams was totally focused on being successful, of only winning. His future wife, in looking at the big picture of athletics, considered more than the success of winning: She considered the possibility that he could be significant to the sport itself. I argue that his total focus on success kept him from becoming a significant runner, yet her significant force in his life led to his becoming one of the most successful British runners in Olympic history.

PERSONAL JOURNEY TOWARD SIGNIFICANCE

U2's song "I Still Haven't Found What I'm Looking For" is about someone who seems to have everything but who is not happy because he still has not found happiness in the material possessions that he has. The song was very meaningful for me because its lyrics gave voice to what I was feeling at one time in my career. I was unhappy as a teacher and a coach. In retrospect, I now know that as a young coach, I was just trying to be successful. I wanted my athletic teams to win games and I wanted my English students to do well on the Texas Assessment of Knowledge and Skills (TAKS). Relationships with students came secondary to my individual success.

EDUCATIONAL GRACE

Over time, I changed to more of a relationship philosophy. At least I thought I had changed. A little over one year ago, if anyone had told me that I still was not grounded in relationship philosophy, I would have seriously argued the point.

However, in my doctoral studies, we studied the work of Margaret Wheatley and Paulo Freire, two authors whose works have begun a transformation in my philosophy of relationships. In her seminal work *Leadership and the New Science*, Margaret Wheatley (1999) argues, "We live in a world where relationships are primary. Nothing happens in the quantum world without something encountering something else. Nothing exists independent of its relationships. We are constantly creating the world—evoking it from many potentials—as we participate in all its many interactions" (p. 69). Relationships are not built on my terms, but on the terms of others. Every time I step into the hallway during a class change or walk into a teacher's room or lead a faculty meeting I am encountering others and causing interactions, which impact relationships.

Paulo Freire (1998) reminds us in his important book *Pedagogy of Freedom*, "What makes men and women ethical is their capacity to 'spiritualize' the world, to make it either beautiful or ugly" (p. 53). I began to consider that one way to see the world in this way is through the concept of "grace." Lyrics from another of U2's songs, "Grace," made this even clearer to me:

> Grace makes beauty out of ugly things;
> Grace finds beauty in everything;
> Grace finds goodness in everything.

In reflecting on my growth in the area of relationships over the past year, I have noticed almost faith-like convictions that are being fine-tuned. To be more than merely a successful educator is to be a significant educator. There is a form of educational grace that must restructure my foundational philosophy about the significant role of relationships in the educational profession. Two key questions must be answered about educational grace: What is it? and, What should it look like when we apply it to our students?

GRACE IS NOT EARNED

"Grace" is defined in *Webster's New Collegiate Dictionary* as a disposition to be generous or helpful; goodwill mercy; clemency; a favor rendered by one who need not do so, indulgence; freely bestowed love and protection. Applying this definition to the educational profession, we know that educational grace is not something our students should ever have to earn. Giving something freely is a foreign idea to many of us because we live in a society that is based on earnings and rewards. Certainly, I have earned the grades that I have received in my graduate work. Further, I am working full-time so that I can continue to earn a paycheck.

In the business world, employee performance is paramount to the rewards of the company. Ford employees are categorized on a scale of 1 to 27. Category "1" would be given to clerks and secretaries. Individuals must reach category 9 to receive an outside parking place. Category 13 brings with it such perks as a window, plants, and an intercom system. Category 16 offices come equipped with private bathrooms. Category 27 is reserved for the chairman of the board. All Ford rewards are based on its employees' performance for the company. With Ford, employees get what they earn.

Yet grace is a gift, free of charge, unexpected, undeserved. No gift is needed in return; it is absolutely unconditional. Grace in the school setting would mean that students should not have to earn help from educators. I clearly remember sitting in my English I classroom as a ninth-grade student trying to struggle through *A Tale of Two Cities*. I really was not giving much effort because I just knew that I would hate the book, so why even try to read it! My teacher, Mrs. Simmons, was very challenging and very demanding. Yet when she observed my reluctance to read the book, she did not respond in an authoritarian manner. Rather, she responded with a gesture of grace—she gently put her hand on my shoulder and said, "Jim, you are a strong reader, and smart students like you find that they enjoy this book once they get through the first few pages." I was not a strong reader at the time nor was I a particularly smart student, but I did have potential to improve in both areas. Mrs. Simmons' grace, a completely undeserved compliment, and faith that I possessed intelligence that she had not yet seen are the reasons I enjoy reading today and why I have remained a lifelong learner.

GRACE GIVES ANOTHER CHANCE

Life rarely allows second chances, but educational grace allows students second, third, or even fourth chances. We never give up on students, even when they might give up on themselves. My youngest son, Trey, and his good friend Brock play a very complex game in our backyard. I have watched them for hours and still do not understand the rules of the game. When one of them violates a "rule," the other one calls him on it, and the offender is out of the game. However, all the losing person has to do to reenter the game is call for a "do over" and all sins are forgiven. The game starts over with no repercussions for prior mistakes.

Our campus's crisis counselor, Jimmy Branch, is a longtime educator and was a very successful principal, but his true passion is working with kids in crisis. He came out of retirement to join our staff and share his passion with our students and staff. He has one rule in golf: If you can get to your tee shot before it stops rolling, it does not count as a stroke. You get to pick that shot up, put it back on the tee, and hit another drive. You get a "do over." I have used that "do over" in golf more times than

I really want to admit, yet just the knowledge that I will get a free shot or two during a round of golf allows me to enjoy the game more than I would if I had to take every one of my shots seriously. It gives me hope that I may have an enjoyable round.

If we demand perfection from our students at all times, we add tremendous pressure to their lives. We take away their hope, and, according to Freire (1998), "the absence of hope is not the normal way to be human" (p. 69). We give our children hope when they know they have a "do over" and sometimes a third or even a fourth chance. Children should not be expected to be perfect.

EQUALITY OF GRACE

Finally, educational grace is open to all students on an equal basis. According to Rachels (2003), "from the moral point of view, there are no privileged persons" (p. 13). Therefore, each of us must acknowledge that other people's welfare is just as important as our own. I am reminded of a cartoon I saw recently: Calvin and Hobbes are walking along and Calvin says, "You know what the problem is with the universe?"

Hobbes responds, "What?"

Calvin answers, "There's no toll-free customer service hot line for complaints! That's why things don't get fixed. If the universe had any decent management, we'd get a full refund if we weren't completely satisfied!"

Hobbes objects, "But hey, the universe is free."

Calvin retorts, "See, that's another thing. The universe should have a cover charge and keep out all the riffraff."

Public education does not have a cover charge and makes no effort to either identify anyone as riffraff or keep them out of school. There are schools where students who do not pass the standards of a rigorous entrance examination are not allowed to attend. Students with behavior difficulties, learning disabilities, or financial limitations are often not allowed to matriculate to these exclusive schools. Yet most public schools have no screening process. We educate all students, no matter what their standing or educational motivation.

CHAPTER 7

FUTURE POTENTIAL IS UNKNOWN

Educational grace means that we should never write a student off because we never know what greatness lies behind our students. Consider the story of John Newton.

John Newton, who lived in the 1800s, was described as a naval deserter, a willing slave trader, a profane infidel, a libertine, and a blasphemer. In fact, he had a reputation for a level of debauchery such that even hardened sailors were surprised by his behavior. During one of his trips home, the boat he was on encountered a terrible storm, and it became doubtful that he or anyone else on the ship would survive the journey and might die at sea. The storm raged for many days, and Newton was even tied to the helm to keep from being washed away by the fierceness of the wind and waves. During his struggle to save himself and the others on the boat, Newton asked the Lord for mercy, and he survived the storm.

Newton struggled to understand why he had been spared. How could someone who had lived such a terrible life be the recipient of the Lord's grace? He eventually dedicated himself to a Christian life and became a prolific writer and penned the hymn originally titled "Faith's Review and Expectation," which contained the following lyrics:

> Amazing grace! (how sweet the sound)
> That sav'd a wretch like me!
> I once was lost, but now am found,
> Was blind, but now I see.

If a blasphemer, an infidel, and a man whose actions were so vile that hardened sailors were shocked at his level of debauchery can overcome his past to write such wonderful music, then how can we, as educators, ever make assumptions about the future capabilities of our students with any degree of certainty? The only certainty is that we can never know what potential lies buried within our students' hearts.

If grace truly does find beauty in everything, then my job as an educator is to find beauty in ninth graders who are lost in a sense or who are temporarily blinded by adolescence. My job is to help them see, and I can do that by grace.

BILL'S STORY

At one of our pep rallies this school year, I looked up into the crowd during the National Anthem and noticed three students sitting down and not participating. These students were dressed in the Gothic manner, and I immediately went into the stands and removed them from the gym. As we were walking to the classroom that serves as our in-school suspension room, I was very angry and asked Bill, the leader of this small group, why they were not participating. His response was that they were exercising their right not to participate in the pep rally. I became even angrier and informed him that I was going to exercise my right as principal to not let them attend any more pep rallies. As I was walking away, Bill said, "That's fine with us. We don't want to be there anyway."

The next day, in my graduate class, we were studying *Subtractive Schooling* by Angela Valenzuela (1999). During our discussion, the following quote resonated for me: "What looks to teachers and administrators like opposition and lack of caring, feels to students like powerlessness and alienation" (p. 94). Bill and his friends did not want to go to our pep rally. Athletics, cheerleaders, and dance squads are not relevant to him or his group, yet his principal (me) was forcing them to attend with an expectation that they participate. They felt powerless and alienated, and I mistakenly viewed it as oppositional behavior.

The following Monday, I found Bill during lunch and asked him if I could join his game of hacky sack. After haplessly trying to keep that ball in the air for more than one try, I asked for his suggestions for an option other than mandatory attendance at the pep rally. On the day of the next pep rally, we opened the library for Bill and his friends who did not want to go. A group of about 25 students went to the library and read, played hacky sack, or studied. All of those students were the ones who brought negative energy to previous pep rallies, yet they were very happy in the library. The pep rally was actually much better too. Only those who wanted to be there were there. The next day, several of Bill's friends thanked me for not making them attend the pep rally.

This seemingly small gesture was profound in its results. Bill's group had input into their educational experience. They were not being forced to support an extracurricular activity that did not appeal to them. Listening to their suggestion had taken away a large portion of their alienation toward the school experience and toward school personnel. Bill and I played an awful lot of hacky sack the remainder of the year and I even kept it in the air for two hits one time.

SUCCESSFUL TRYOUTS OR A SIGNIFICANT EXPERIENCE

I have yet to see anything in education as painful, emotional, and tear inducing as cheerleader tryouts. It seems that failure to make cheerleader is a rejection of athletic ability, beauty, and popularity, of one's total being. It is a grueling process and one of the least favorite activities that I am required to administrate. In our school, those who want to try out are given a tryout number. They learn a common cheer and then are put on display both as an individual and in a small group to do the cheer. Judges hired from outside the community have no prior knowledge of the students. At the end of the tryout, the students and their parents leave until the results are calculated.

Two hours later, we post the list of numbers selected. The students come back and look for their number so it is common to have one student crying and another jumping for joy. The girls and boys who do not make cheerleader experience a sense of rejection seemingly deeper than any other activity in schools. As an administrator, I have a responsibility not to just settle for a successful cheerleader election. My job is to make the whole process significant so that those who do not earn a place on the squad are treated with grace and compassion, and they leave the experience with their dignity intact. This year, I tried to accomplish that goal by writing the following letter to each girl and boy who did not get selected:

Dear Melinda:

I wanted you to know how proud I am of you for trying out for our cheerleading squad, and I know that you are probably feeling some disappointment right now. Those are natural feelings, and I have experienced them myself. As a young coach, it took me four years of trying before I was able to get a head coaching position. As a young administrator, it took me several tries before I was able to become a principal. One of my favorite quotes is an old Chinese proverb, "If you fall seven times, rise eight." So I kept trying, and eventually, I was successful.

It takes a lot of courage to make the decision to even try out for something like cheerleader. The fact that you made the decision to become involved shows me that you are a leader on your campus and you truly care about making our school a better place. We have many opportunities at the Ninth Grade Center for our students to become involved, including Blue Belles, student council, athletics, a model airplane club, the Geo Club, choir, band, teen leadership, and many more. I hope that you will choose to become involved in some of those because we need leaders like you in those activities. In fact, if we do not have a club for something that you are interested in, we will consider starting a new one with you as a founding member.

Melinda, I am looking forward to having you on this campus and being your principal. If you ever need anything or if I can ever help you, please let me know.

Sincerely,

The purpose of this letter was to encourage the students who did not make cheerleader to become involved in other activities. More importantly, I wanted them to know that someone knew that they had taken a risk and tried. At our school, we also decided to modify our process by announcing the results of the cheerleader elections on our website so that the girls and boys could find out the results in the privacy of their homes. Just having successful cheerleading elections is not enough; we must be significant in helping that experience be less traumatic for our students.

CONCLUSION

I have determined from my many years in education that there are really two kinds of educators—those who want to be successful and those who want to be significant. While it is possible for one to be a successful educator without being significant, it is not possible to be significant without being successful. With many of the readings and class discussions in the doctoral studies serving as a catalyst, I now recognize that often goals of individual success are selfish and are not shared with others. Yet if I establish goals that extend grace to help others, I will make a significant, shared contribution to their success. When students come to my office, I now view them as unfinished projects that do not have to earn my help. I will use educational grace as I assist them along the journey. To be successful in this profession and as a human being, all I need to do is be significant by helping our students. If I am significant, I will be successful.

Jim Vaszauskas is principal of the Ninth Grade Center in Weatherford Independent School District.

8

MY JOURNEY ON THE YELLOW BRICK ROAD

Sharon Young

> Maybe you've been afraid to make a career move. If you've known in your heart that you should have changed jobs or started a new business, now is the time to face up to it. . . . If it's the right thing to do, then do it.
>
> —J. C. Maxwell (1999, p. 43)

All other class members had completed their presentations; now it was my turn. It was easy for me to stand in front of my class and teach, but I was terrified of speaking in front of my peers. My head was hurting, and my stomach was tied in knots. I went into the hallway and cried. I wanted to quit! I was certain that I had started something that I could not finish. I could not breathe; fear clutched me so tightly that as I tried to speak, my voice quivered and was barely over a whisper. For the first time in my life, I was going to fail! I had never failed at anything in my life, but this was going to be the first time! I had returned to school to get my master's degree, but was it worth all of this?

These feelings returned to me three years later as I sat in an interview for the position of elementary principal. I wanted to make sure the board members were able to see my desire to get this job and to do it well. Near the end of the interview, the superintendent looked at me and asked if I had anything else that I would like to add. I looked up slowly, took a deep breath, and opened my mouth to speak. I still do not know where the words came from at that particular moment, but I looked at him and then at each board member in turn and said, "All I ask is that you give me a chance. I may not have the experience that the other candidates have, but I have a desire to do what is best for children. I know I can do this job and do it well. Please, just give me a chance." Three days later I received the call that would change my life; they had taken a chance on me. I was offered the job to be the elementary principal.

INTRODUCTION

Two years ago, when I entered the doctoral program, I thought I had my career goals etched in stone. I dreamed, as Dorothy had at the beginning of the *Wizard of Oz*, of a land where everything was beautiful. I was going to follow the yellow brick road from teacher to assistant principal, then move up to the principal position so that once there I would be able to provide all the answers to those I perceived to be in need of enlightenment. I had set out in search of my dream by earning a master's degree. As I looked for a future in the Emerald City of educational leadership, I was content letting other people lead me into what I needed to know and content with the amount of knowledge that I was receiving. When I earned my master's degree, I felt that I had finished the amount of education I thought was necessary to be a principal. Knowledge could not, however, make up for a lack of confidence. I needed something more than just pure academic knowledge. I was in need of an inner strength that at that time I did not possess. For two years after passing my principal's exam, I did not attempt to interview for administrative jobs. I was afraid to be responsible for making the decisions that would impact the lives of an entire campus of students.

Entering a doctoral program lifted me up and set me down in a land that was beautiful and colorful. I felt like Dorothy as she dropped with the house into the land of the munchkins! My world had gone from black and white to Technicolor. I had told myself in the past that I needed to accept that I was a teacher, and that was all that I was going to be. But, as I entered the doctoral program, I felt that the house had dropped on my wicked witch of self-doubt. I realized that I *did* possess the knowledge necessary to sit in the same classroom with administrators and other educational leaders. At that instant, however, I knew I still had one more witch to defeat. That witch embodied the lack of confidence that I had the ability to be successful in an administrative position. Just as the house dropped on the witch of self-doubt, I felt confident that one day my bucket of knowledge would be full. I would be able to use it to melt away the lack of confidence that I had in myself. It would take a full year for me to develop a sense of confidence that would give me the courage to take the risks that must be taken to step away from a nice, comfortable teaching job into a challenging, new administrative career.

In the *Wizard of Oz*, Dorothy traveled down the yellow brick road with three companions in search of the wizard who would help her return to her family. My journey toward my doctoral degree has been similar; however, I find the companions are not entities unto themselves, but actually a part of me. Like Dorothy, I use the attributes for which her companions the scarecrow, the tin man, and lion searched. My educational leadership embodies knowledge, feeling, and courage. I use the latest, research-based theories regarding curriculum, instruction, and leadership to guide my practice. However, in the educational field, I cannot lead with mere knowledge because this kind of leadership does not embody feeling. Education is not a cold, sterile field—it involves the lives of students on an ongoing basis. However, leading strictly with the heart is very difficult in this time of accountability. Courage helps me to speak out about what I feel is right, but at the same time, I must possess knowledge, which provides a strong, theoretical base for these courageous actions, as well as feeling, which allows me to focus on students' individual needs in relation to issues of equity and social justice.

As I reflect on the journey that I have traveled up to this point in my educational endeavors, the story of the *Wizard of Oz* has become a metaphor for my journey since I have been enrolled in a doctoral program. The professors in the program have resembled Glenda, the good witch. I have entered into their magical world, and through their guidance, I have been able to learn and to acquire new knowledge of my inner self. Although at times I have wanted my professors to just tell me what to do and how to do it, I realize that the knowledge for which I am searching cannot come solely from any external source. This knowledge must come from my personal experiences as I acquire new knowledge, reflect on it, and apply it to my practice as a scholar-practitioner leader. At the same time, I must rely on the guidance of my teachers; often their direction down the path of exploration has kept me from straying too far from the path of knowledge required in a new world of transformative education.

SEARCHING FOR KNOWLEDGE

Just as the scarecrow searched for a brain, I have looked for knowledge and theoretical grounding by studying different educational philosophies that would be the basis for my growth as a scholar-practitioner. It is no longer acceptable for me to do the right thing; I need to understand why I make certain decisions based on pragmatic inquiry. As an educational leader, I cannot be content with the knowledge that I possess. I am challenged to learn more and to apply that knowledge to my practice while constantly reevaluating the results of my practice. Schools are ever changing. Just using a brain is not the end for the scarecrow or for me; it is merely the beginning of a new base of knowledge for continued study. I am acquiring a knowledge base, but it is up to me to have the courage and confidence to continue to learn in preparation for my future as an educational leader.

The first day I walked into my new office as elementary principal, I was proud of my new position and ready to make a difference. It did not take me long to realize that I was going to have to use the knowledge I had gained over the past few years to get everything in order. My new school was a very small school with 230 students, located in a rural community of East Texas. It had not had a designated elementary principal for the preceding two years. When I arrived at the school, I discovered that the requisitions had not been filled for the upcoming year, questions regarding the placement of students needed to be answered, and the school was at risk of losing a grant if specific staff development was not completed quickly. What was I to do? Where did I begin? I had the knowledge necessary to look at the requisitions and determine if the material needed would be beneficial to the success of the students. I also had the knowledge of state laws regarding the promotion and placement of students into the next grade. The staff development was not something that I needed to present myself, but it did require my encouragement and support for the teachers who would be involved in this process.

As a doctoral student, I have acquired grounding in scholarly theory, and I also have learned the practical knowledge of setting priorities and managing time. In my new position as an elementary principal, I frequently take a step back and look at the situations in turn, engaging in careful reflection on the many ramifications of my decisions before I make them. When I first arrived at my new school, in order to ensure that the school was able to receive its grant funding, the teachers and I spent the next two days working together to finish the staff development. I knew that I wanted to be a facilitative leader who would work with teachers in a collaborative process, rather than an authoritative one who would mandate decisions without consideration of others' needs. I wanted the teachers to have ownership in the staff development activities.

In addition, I met with the Campus Placement Committee to review individual academic progress over the past academic year, as well as social, emotional, and behavioral issues regarding individual students, in order to determine if students would be eligible to be promoted to the next grade. After dealing with these issues, I turned my attention to the folder that was full of requests that teachers had made at the end of the school year. With less than a week before school started, there were not enough funds to order everything requested. With my newfound confidence, I looked through the requests and selected what was essential for student success. After ordering those items, I went through all the supply closets, moving leftover supplies into my office. I took the supplies and made a bag for each teacher to begin the school year. Although I had not actively been involved in building the shared vision of the campus, I followed the "tactical actions" suggested by Harris (2004, pp. 11–12). It was this knowledge of building relationships through supporting needs that provided me a nearly perfect first week of school. Because of my experience in the doctoral program, my confidence in myself was growing. This allowed me to integrate my theoretical knowledge with the common sense of practice to solve the problems that would have overwhelmed me in the past.

SEARCHING FOR HEART

Just like the tin man, I search for a heart as I continue to work through the issues related to democratic leadership. I am trying to engage in a leadership practice that is socially just to all those whom I encounter. I have experienced a transformational process during the last few years in my continued learning, which has helped prepare me for effective scholar-practitioner leadership, and I have developed a personal conviction to do what I think is right and just. Inspired by the readings of such theorists as Freire (1998) and Sergiovanni (1992), I realize that I must lead from the heart and for the betterment of the students. I am finding that just as Freire (1998) suggested, "Sometimes a simple, almost insignificant gesture on the part of a teacher can have a profound formative effect on the life of a student" (p. 46). Can one person change the culture of a nation or the face of the educational system? The answer to that question is "no"; however, my confidence is growing as I realize that I can make a difference on my campus. This confidence will encourage teachers and students to make a difference in the lives of the people with whom they come in contact, and the cycle of acceptance and tolerance will grow and lives will change.

As the ethic of care is practiced in the educational setting, there are a few areas at my new school that require intense consideration. One area where I have chosen to focus is the success of special education students. Special needs students are often placed in separate rooms to receive instruction, and these rooms become "schools within schools," where large numbers of culturally and academically diverse students are segregated. In these educationally restrictive settings, special needs students receive very little socialization with their non-disabled students in the mainstream education setting. In addition, they are often denied access to grade-level curriculum and instructional educational opportunities. As an educational leader, I must set an example for teachers that encourages them to provide instructional accommodations to special needs students in general education settings. This will enable these students to experience opportunities to socialize with their grade level peers and to be exposed to grade-level curriculum and instruction. Supporting teachers to provide these students with the extra instructional assistance that they need to experience academic success will strengthen our learning community. However, in the past, the school's only option for special needs students has been to send them into a full resource setting, which means that they spend the majority of their instructional day socially and academically separated from their peers. I attempted to change this educational practice at my new elementary school.

Before school started, I met with the special education teachers and asked for their input regarding how to allow the students to remain in general educational settings for a greater percentage of the day. Teachers were familiar with the educational practice of a content mastery room that is implemented at other schools to allow special needs students to remain in the classroom with their non-disabled peers and to leave only for additional help needed after they acquire instruction from their general education teachers. Since the special education teachers and I were afraid of how the general education teachers would react to keeping these students in their classrooms for a larger portion of the day, we asked the general education teachers to keep all special needs students in their classrooms for the first two days of school to provide the special needs students with opportunities to interact with their non-disabled grade-level peers. At the end of these two days, we met as a faculty to discuss the concept of the content mastery room. To my surprise, the regular education teachers were very supportive of the plan, and many of them voiced their desire to keep the students in their classes as much as possible. I realized that these teachers did indeed have the heart and ethic of care to meet the needs of the special needs students—they had just never been given the opportunity to demonstrate these attributes!

Just as the tin man received a heart to experience feeling, I must use my own heart to make decisions based on care and compassion as an educational leader. Now that I have confidence in my ethic of care, I must apply it to educational and community settings so that every child, teacher, and community member is treated with compassion. I can now say I truly have a heart and the confidence to make decisions based on what is right!

SEARCHING FOR COURAGE

Dorothy's final traveling partner was the cowardly lion who was searching for courage. As the lion, I knew that I needed to find the courage necessary to be a practitioner who is authentic and interested in building a community that works together through collaboration and shared respect. My goal is to develop an educational system that will work for the end result of success for all students. I understand that as Duffy (2003) stated, "Courageous, passionate, and visionary leaders in school districts need to recognize that their effectiveness as change-leaders is the result of skillful interplay of power, politics, and ethics" (p. 18). Duignan and Bhindi (1997) challenged leaders to remain true to their personal values and use those values as a foundation to develop relationships that are both "human and humane. . . . The leader's relationship to followers must be at all times authentic" (p. 207). This authentic relationship combined with the practice of critical inquiry will benefit the students, and it will facilitate the trust of all involved.

When I accepted the position of elementary principal, I knew that I would have to find the courage to approach the teachers regarding an area that was in need of drastic improvement. The school had fallen below the state average in almost every area of accountability. As a leader, I needed to address a plan of action that, while courageous in the presentation of areas that were weak in the school's curriculum, would not be viewed by my staff members as belittling. I prepared a presentation for each grade, focusing on the student test data for their assigned grade level and the grade level below them. I did not know how the teachers would react to having a new principal attempt to explain how to improve their test scores, so I approached the situation in a very different way than the one that my previous principals had used. I did not say anything about improving test scores but, instead, I asked questions aimed at specific test questions that had been missed by the majority of the students. The teachers began to discuss different questions. The conversations were full of collaboration between the different grade levels regarding how they could assist one another to better meet their students' needs. I had feared the teachers' reactions, but I was delighted with their willingness to share ideas and concerns. The next day, a kindergarten teacher came into my office to ask for materials that were supportive of the third-grade test. She was already working to integrate into her curriculum material that would help her students experience more academic success!

I would be wrong if I tried to take credit for creating the sense of community in this school. However, my confidence to ask the teachers to look at test data in a different way and to determine the best solution for "our" school was an important step in building this new community. This new learning community, as well as my leadership that embodies courage and authenticity, will be a part of a collaborative environment that concentrates on the simple goal of doing what is best for the students on our campus. I have found in myself the courage to make a difference.

THE JOURNEY CONTINUES

Just as Dorothy entered the Kingdom of Oz, I experienced a new feeling of confidence as I entered my job as elementary principal. Even though in the first week of this experience I said many times, "This may work today but blow up in our faces tomorrow," I had the confidence to take these risks. I realize that my knowledge is incomplete and that it will remain incomplete for the rest of my life. If I do not continue to learn, then I will not continue to walk the yellow brick road toward Emerald City, where all students are successful. In my quest in this growing process, I will travel through decades of studies, looking for the answers to my deepest desires to overcome personal and professional challenges.

I challenge myself to become a leader who will combine the knowledge of the scarecrow after he acquired his brain, the ethic of care of the tin man after he acquired his heart, the confidence of the lion after he acquired his courage, and the knowledge of self obtained by Dorothy as she encountered adventures in the land of Oz. When I finally finish this journey down my yellow brick road toward the Emerald City and return home, I will engage in other journeys down other roads less traveled.

I began this chapter by describing a presentation that terrified me. It was that fear and lack of confidence that led me down this path in search of my inner self. Yet, encouraged by Sergiovanni (1992), "the heart of leadership has to do with what a person believes, values, dreams about, and is committed to. . . . The head of leadership is shaped by the heart and drives the hand; in turn, reflections on decisions and actions affirm or reshape the heart and the head" (p. 7), I know I am on the right road. As I began my journey, I put on ruby slippers that symbolized my desire to find knowledge and confidence. I have found some knowledge and more confidence than I had at the beginning of this journey, but I realize now that I will be wearing these slippers for a very long time, for my journey down the yellow brick road is not yet over.

Sharon Young is an elementary principal at Kennard Independent School District in Kennard, Texas.

EMPOWERMENT: THE QUICKENING

Logan Faris

> Humanity has waited an eternity for me and the unique possibilities and potential I have and can offer to humanity.
>
> —Robert Starratt

> Kids are defeated inch by inch or encouraged inch by inch. How do students leave your campus? With an inch of defeat or encouragement?
>
> —Robert Starratt

DEVELOPING LEADERSHIP PERCEPTIONS

My teaching and administrative experiences have contributed to form my personal perception of the purpose of education and the role of the participants. However, my educational preferences and practices continue to evolve as my awareness and philosophy of education evolves. This philosophy is grounded in a combination of the experience I have gained as a student, teacher, and administrator. I have been constantly reminded as a teacher to remember my perceptions as a student, and to remember as an administrator my perceptions as a teacher. As I have cultivated an understanding of the diverse and interconnected needs of students, parents, teachers, and administrators, I have worked to implement this understanding in a manner that encourages empowerment at all levels. This process of implementing effective practices based on my developing understanding should manifest itself as leadership. Leadership then emerges as the conduit by which our perceptions are animated. As we execute our beliefs and perceptions through our practices, we bring our beliefs to life. Therefore, our leadership can only be as strong as our understanding of the practices being implemented.

STUDENTS' PERCEPTION OF EMPOWERMENT

In the fall of 1975, I reported for kindergarten to begin my educational experience. My novice senses were immediately inundated with stimuli from this new environment. I can still vividly recall the smell of new clothes and shoes mingled with chalk dust and Elmer's glue, the feel of well-worn carpet under my feet and a Big Chief writing tablet under the heel of my hand, the sound of lunch trays and utensils in a cafeteria and the opening and closing of the sliding school bus door, the taste of milk from a paper carton and salty sweat from playing on the playground, the vivid colors of the decorations in the classroom and the glimmering welcoming smile of a friendly teacher. These stimuli imprinted within me and began to create a personal perspective of education and its value through my own personal experiences. Each subsequent year began similarly with the assimilation of a new classroom, teacher, and classmates to the increasing familiarity I was gaining with the overall educational setting. These familiar stimuli contributed to my comfort and allowed me to develop the basic fundamentals of my education. This process continued as I progressed through the elementary and middle school grades. Big Chief writing tablets gave way to college-ruled notebook paper and the dig of a backpack into my shoulder.

I basked in the light of an all-star cast of teachers in both elementary and middle school who provided a plentiful dose of encouragement and empowerment. However, my freshman year in high school included an event that changed my life. I was enrolled in a regular ninth-grade English class taught by Mrs. Ferguson. The year was filled with stimulating instruction that was engaging and exciting due to the dynamic relationship I developed with my English teacher. I found myself devoting additional time and effort to my studies to fulfill my desire to please Mrs. Ferguson. As a result, I developed into a strong and creative writer.

Mrs. Ferguson was able to identify and nurture potential in me that I had not been able to recognize. Our relationship forged a culture of encouragement and empowerment I had never experienced. The spring semester concluded with my receiving the outstanding freshman English award presented by Mrs. Ferguson. I was elated and promptly urged by her to enroll in an advanced English course as a sophomore to further develop my writing skills in a more rigorous setting. Still confident from her accolade, I readily accepted the challenge. This interaction resulted in my enrollment and success in sophomore honors English, as well as honors history, advanced math, and advanced science. Mrs. Ferguson's encouragement and affirmation resulted in my empowerment and eventual graduation with honors from high school, including the completion of six college hours of freshman English as a high school senior via dual credit.

The confidence and encouragement I gained in school prepared me for a successful college career. The years continued to slip by almost silently, and I soon found myself as a college graduate, transitioning into the next phase of my educational experience . . . this time as a teacher.

TEACHERS' PERCEPTION OF EMPOWERMENT

My educational journey as a learner now added the perspective of classroom teacher. As a teacher, I soon realized the importance of an education and the impact a teacher can have on students' lives. The diversity of student skills and needs began to further mold my educational perspectives. After teaching a short time, I experienced a series of life-changing events. One profound event in particular occurred when my teaching assignment included coaching the baseball team in a small rural school. David was a student in my class who had severe learning disabilities and did not participate in any extracurricular activities. He struggled in all his classes and had already fallen behind in earning his high school credits. David was truly an at-risk student.

One crisp February morning, our science class was walking along a nearby logging road observing animal tracks when David and I began throwing rocks from alongside the logging road. I was impressed with David's power and accuracy in hitting trees with the rocks being thrown. I asked him if he had ever played baseball and he passively shrugged his shoulders and replied, "No." I then asked if he had a baseball glove, to which he again passively replied, "No." I told him that I would like for him to come out after school and throw a baseball with our team. He reluctantly agreed and I was thrilled to see him report to the baseball field that afternoon. I provided him a glove and sent him with Charles, my starting catcher, to the bullpen to throw and warm up his arm. Charles quietly protested to me and complained that David was "too dumb" for our baseball team. I quickly reprimanded him and asked him to trust me; then he hustled to the bullpen to throw with David. I went about my drills with the rest of the team and proceeded with our practice.

Shortly after resuming practice I was interrupted by an almost frantic Charles urging me to come with him to the bullpen. Not sure of his intent, I hurried with him to see why he was so excited. As we reached the bullpen, Charles said, "Dude, watch this!" and quickly took his place behind the plate. "OK, David! Show Coach what you've got!" With that, David hurled a perfect strike that popped the catcher's mitt, sending a cloud of dust flying. When I looked at David and praised him, I noticed that his face was glowing with pride. This incident won over the entire team, and, with a crash course in pitching, David soon took his place as our prized relief pitcher.

This affirmed to me the potential that can be realized when students and teachers are empowered with confidence and encouragement. The real reward in this situation was that David was interacting with his peers in an extracurricular activity, which led him to begin passing his classes in order to continue to participate with the baseball team. Teachers are able to build capacities in their students in a way that few others in their life can. I learned that we often underestimate the impact of teachers. Vasquez-Levy and Timmerman (2000) affirmed, "Teachers are the greatest resource, not only because there are so many of them, but, because of the influence they can have on school-level problems" (p. 368). This is a perspective that I also have found to be true. Teachers are closest to students and are in an effective position to assess their needs. I discovered that this relationship should be the foundation and motivation for empowering teachers. Teachers make daily contact with their students and are in the constant process of investing in their education and lives. Teachers become invaluable experts that possess both personal and professional wisdom. Through teacher empowerment, we can begin to tap this resource and make it available for realizing the successful education of all students.

LEADERS' PERCEPTION OF EMPOWERMENT

Despite enjoying teaching and coaching, I felt an urge to move from the classroom into a campus-level administrative position. The urge was fed by the desire to support and empower teachers and students campuswide. Just as when I became a teacher, this transition created a new perspective. In agreement with Fullan (2001), who avowed that "good leaders foster good leadership at other levels" (p. 10), I quickly realized the impact an administrator can have on the faculty of a campus when teachers are encouraged and empowered.

Kim was a first-year teacher who was part of a very dysfunctional social studies department. Her first semester was characterized by the typical student conflicts and was also littered with negative colleagues and uncooperative parents. At the close of the fall semester, I found her in the curriculum office at her wit's end. She was completely frustrated and felt as though she had no one to whom she could turn for help. After consoling Kim, I recommended that she be a part of our campus climate committee. She agreed and began reporting to our meetings.

After a couple of months of participating with the climate committee, Kim began to gain confidence and felt as though she was making improvements despite her negative environment. She was excited to meet each time with her new committee because they provided her with a forum to discuss campus needs and a new set of mentors who supported her with encouragement and advice. In March, our committee was allowed to attend a three-day state conference where we attended presentations concerning student motivation strategies, campus culture, and a variety of instructional innovations. This conference also provided time for our committee to reflect on presentations and their potential for our campus. It was at this conference that I witnessed Kim emerge and break loose from the negative chains of apathy and frustration.

Upon returning from the conference, Kim no longer allowed this negative environment to dictate her attitude. She had evolved from a discouraged teacher into a neophyte leader with the desire and ability to change her department by modeling positive attitudes and innovative instructional strategies. The department reacted critically but this had no effect on Kim, who now had a source of confidence and empowerment that had been lacking in the fall semester. Before long, some of the apathetic members of her department curiously inquired about her success in the classroom and she was able to become the mentor she had never had.

This equipping should be the goal of administrators who empower teachers. I had simply suggested that Kim join our climate committee and this cultivating environment afforded her with the missing support she needed for success. Kim's experience was an example of Paula Short's (1994) description of the teacher empowerment process "whereby school participants develop the competence to take charge of their own growth and resolve their own problems" (p. 488). I realized that empowerment could produce a self-confident, collaborative collection of educational professionals who can corporately address the myriad challenges facing modern education. Through supporting and encouraging teachers, educational leadership can provide the crucial awareness that an individual can impact and promote the success of the organization.

A single person can make the difference. By modeling successful strategies and providing the resources needed, teachers can become empowered beyond expectation. This ideology is reflected by Short and Rinehart (1992) when they declared, "Teachers who perceive a greater sense of empowerment believe that they impact the work of the organization. . . . It is reasonable to expect empowered teachers to assume ownership of organizational problems and their solutions" (p. 595). Fullan (2001) further identified the potential of teacher empowerment when he stated,

> Collaborative cultures are indeed powerful, but unless they are focusing on the right things they may end up being powerfully wrong. Moral pur-

pose, good ideas, focusing on results, and obtaining the views of dissenters are essential, because they mean that the organization [school] is focusing on the right things. (p. 67–68).

This statement captures my developing perception of the true potential of teacher empowerment and identifies the need for educational leadership to help nurture and guide the empowerment process. Once teachers develop ownership in the school and individual commitment begins to take root, then the school can realize true and sustainable success.

FUTURE PERCEPTIONS

Freire (1998) introduces the concept of "unfinishedness" to describe the human condition. As a leader and educator, I can relate to this descriptor. As I reflect back over the last 30 years of my life, I can sense a pattern: continuous education. Beginning in kindergarten, I have experienced times of slow and gentle progress interrupted with times of intense quickening where experience and practicality collide to generate synthesis. This pattern of continuous learning confirms to me that I am "unfinished" and lack much in my life professionally and personally. This last year as a doctoral student has proven to be my most intense and productive quickening thus far.

My perception of empowering leadership has undergone subtle transformation as I have moved from student to teacher to administrator. This transformation has been quickened with my recent practical and theoretical studies in educational leadership. I am now able to ground my experiences and values, such as empowerment, in proven research. As I reflect back on the past year in the doctoral experience, I relate to that of a common oak sapling planted in a small pot in a quaint nursery. My small but numerous fibrous roots were straining against the confines of the small pot, which limited both the potential of the roots system and the visible growth above ground. The familiar confines of the small pot provided security and protection at the price of unrestrained growth.

Today, I find myself transplanted into a new, wide-open space, absent the constraints and securities afforded by the small pot in which I had previously been nurtured and cared for as a seedling. I have now been released to send tendrils deep into the fertile earth and strengthen them into a powerful anchor and source of nourishment. The cultivation of this underground network will soon be evident in the quickly paced production of visible trunk, limb, and leaf. With time, a mature tree will stand and yield fruit where the sapling once stood. This mighty oak will have a firm and grounded foundation comprised of roots both large and small that confidently allow the tree to withstand storms that may arise. This grounded network will make possible many years of growth and reproduction, which will ensure future successful generations to follow. Thus, my growth is quickened as an administrator and as a doctoral student.

Logan Faris is assistant principal for curriculum and instruction at Center High School in Center, Texas.

10

INCLUSION: SOME SOCIAL JUSTICE ISSUES

Sharon Kathleen Ninness

> I prefer to be criticized as an idealist and an inveterate dreamer because I continue to believe in the human person, continue to struggle for legislation that would protect people from the unjust and aggressive inroads of those who have no regard for an ethical code that is common to us all. The freedom of commerce cannot be ethically higher than the freedom to be human. The freedom of commerce without limits is no more than the license to put profit above everything else. It becomes a privilege of the few, who in certain favorable conditions increase their own power at the expense of the greater part of humanity, even to the point of survival itself.
>
> —Paulo Freire (1998, p. 116)

WHO I AM TODAY

When I began my journey as a member of a doctoral cohort, I had no idea how much my life would change. I developed an increased awareness of social justice issues and equity in education as I began to realize that our perspectives of educational issues are influenced by our subjective lenses, which are in turn shaped by social, historical, and cultural contexts. This is the story of my growth in moral philosophy in relation to issues of tracking, ability grouping, and inclusion that I encountered as an educational diagnostician in a small East Texas rural school district.

My doctoral work has included an intensive study of moral philosophy as well as its application to educational policy. This study has incorporated a connection between theory and practice. In an attempt to guide my conduct by reason, I have engaged in much reflection regarding my own moral philosophy. I have tried to attain a systematic understanding of the nature of morality and what it requires of me as an educational leader. This process has involved basing my actions on the best reasons while at the same time giving equal consideration to the interests of individuals who would be affected by these actions. I have striven to make moral judgments that involve both reason and impartiality—decisions that are supported by good reasons and that at the same time impartially consider each individual's interests (Rachels, 1993). Concurring with Rachels' ideas, I understand that the following three conditions work together to make morality both possible and natural for humankind: being impartial, adhering to a set of rules that serve everyone's interests if fairly applied, and caring about others to a certain degree. As an educational leader, I realize that since different people have different merits, it is difficult for humans to promote the interests of everyone in the same manner.

As a result of my studies, ongoing dialogue with my fellow cohort members, intensive reflection, and my own leadership practice, I have developed a wider conception of morality that includes the elements of the promotion of human welfare, justice, and fairness, in addition to the elements of reason and impartiality (Rachels, 1993). I have decided that perhaps the single moral standard is human welfare. Since it is important that people are as happy and well off as possible, this standard of welfare should be used to assess many things, including laws, character traits, and motives. As moral agents, humans should be concerned with people whose welfare might be affected by their actions. All individuals are included in "a community of moral concern" (Rachels, 1993, p. 200), an expansive community that is not limited to people in a particular place or at a particular time. I realize that I must give consideration to the welfare of those worldwide, of future generations, and of all species that inhabit this planet. Justice and fairness also have become important elements of my moral philosophy. These elements must be applied in our society. In a just society, people can improve their positions through work; they do not obtain superior positions based on inherent attributes such as physical beauty and superior intelligence.

I have become an agent of change in a community of moral concern—I have engaged in my own corrective action plan to provide new referrals to special education with the most culturally fair and thorough assessments possible and to implement special education students' individual education plans (IEPs) in the least restrictive environments. As a scholar-practitioner, I have combined the theory of inclusion with my practice as an educational diagnostician, facing many important social justice issues.

I have engaged in ongoing dialogue and intensive reflection regarding various moral perspectives in relation to educational policy, which guides leadership practice. I have become knowledgeable regarding mainstream utilitarianism, rights theories including libertarian and meritocratic perspectives, democratic communitarian thought, and humanistic psychology. After much reflection regarding educational policy in relation to the elements of moral philosophy (reason, impartiality, the promotion of human welfare, justice, and fairness), I have determined that I support a democratic communitarian perspective regarding educational policy.

As a democratic communitarian, I am interested in research that focuses on the unequal and poor-quality instruction students in low tracks receive. I am not impressed with superficial mainstream discussions that connect tracking to democracy. Although the promotion of desegregation and more meritocratic assignments by detracking helps establish more democratic communities, mainstreaming is not the end of the journey to equity. I am troubled by the mainstream emphasis on the desirability of sameness. At the same time, I am critical of mainstream rhetoric that shows little respect for students who would pursue nonacademic priorities. A need exists to consider alternative conceptions of tracking. Efforts to provide all students the same curricula should be criticized. I am aware of the importance of creating curricula that respond to students' interests. At the same time, I have considerations regarding hierarchical and often unequal aspects of current tracking arrangements.

As an advocate of mainstreaming special education students, I recognize the purported injustice of separate placements for special needs students, as well as the invalidity of disability categories, tests, and instructional services associated with special education (Fuchs & Fuchs, 1995). I realize the importance of special needs children making friends with non-disabled classmates—this cannot be accomplished in separate placements. Historically, general education has used special education settings as dumping grounds for students deemed "unteachable," such as those with severe mental retardation. To preclude the stigmatization and warehousing that are inherent in special education classrooms, mainstreaming must occur to the greatest extent possible.

Unfortunately, special education settings have become the moral equivalent of apartheid or slavery (Lipsky & Garner, 1987). Many disability categories, such as learning disabilities, are inventions of educators who seek to rid classrooms of hard-to-teach students, of parents who are seeking additional services for their children, and of special education administrators who desire to expand their special education programs in order to obtain additional federal money (Dillon, 1994). In essence, these disability categories are social constructs that lack scientific validity (Reynolds, 1991). Many invalid tests are used to identify students with exceptional conditions, and as a result, these students are erroneously identified as disabled students and inappropriately placed in special education settings. The most common special education category is learning disability, and many learning disabled students could easily be mainstreamed into general education classrooms.

AN EXPERIENCE FROM MY PAST

Four years ago, the Office of Civil Rights (OCR) visited the small school district where I work as an educational diagnostician. At the time, I was a teacher at one of the elementary schools. Several parents of African American students had filed a complaint that there were a disproportionate number of African American students who were identified as mentally retarded and placed in self-contained classrooms. When the OCR investigated, it found that unfair identification and assessment practices were being used with African American students. Not only were the majority of referrals to special education African American but educational diagnosticians were also using different tests to qualify this population as mentally retarded. In addition, at times, they were using only certain subtests of intelligence tests rather than composite scores (verbal and nonverbal scales as mandated by law) to qualify African American students as mentally retarded. Clearly, this school district was in violation of federal law in its referral and identification processes. The school district was mandated by the OCR to immediately develop a plan of corrective action.

After the OCR visit in 2000, Sunshine Independent School District (ISD) immediately developed a corrective action plan in response to an OCR official report that contained specific recommendations. African American students receiving special education services were to be retested using the same "best practice" testing procedures used with European American students. Each month, the school district had to submit a written report to the OCR stating the number of referrals and their ethnicities, the kinds of tests administered to all new referrals, and the reasons for determination of handicapping conditions for all students who were determined to need special education services. Parts of intelligence tests, other than full verbal, performance, and full scales, could no longer be used to represent students' intelligential functioning.

When I began working as an educational diagnostician for Sunshine ISD shortly after the OCR visit, I encountered some social justice issues related to the district's plan to correct its previous inequitable referral and assessment practices. As a result of intervention from the Office of Civil Rights, school administrators were under pressure to not refer too many African American students to special education. This covert quota resulted in some African American students not getting referred to special education when they had learning problems that were not being adequately remediated by Title I programs, 504 accommodations, and teacher-assistance team interventions.

Over a 12-year period, the district's culturally diverse populations in the elementary schools, where most referrals are made, had significantly increased from 42.7% in 1991 to 72% in 2003. In 1991, 57.3% of the elementary school population was Anglo, 30.9% was African American, 11.2% was Hispanic, and .6% was other (including Asian and Native American populations). Yet, in 2003, 28% of the population in the elementary schools was Anglo, 32.6% was African American, 39% was Hispanic, and .4% was other (Public Education Information Management

System [PEIMS] data). Based on this data, it was not surprising that the majority of new referrals to special education in 2003 came from culturally diverse populations, which comprised the majority of the elementary school population (72%). Educational diagnosticians were mandated to give the same intelligence test, the WISC-III, to each new referral tested, regardless of any considerations such as educational strengths/weaknesses, learning styles, and multiple intelligences. This was not a good practice, as research studies had indicated that African American students' mean IQ on the WISC-III was approximately 13 points lower than that of European American students, and Hispanic students' mean IQ was 9 points lower (Bracken & McCallum, 1998). As Sunshine ISD established a rigorous system of accountability for special education referrals, students' individual differences became ignored.

Two years ago, Sunshine ISD was added to the Texas Education Agency's 125% list. This list includes the names of districts that have 25% over the number of students they should have in more restrictive settings, including self-contained classes, compared to the state average. There were too many students receiving instruction in special education settings for more than 50% of the instructional day, and many of these students were culturally diverse. While the school district had decreased its numbers of culturally diverse students who were identified as mentally retarded, in some cases, this handicapping condition was replaced with one of learning disability after additional testing. A disproportionate number of culturally diverse students identified as having learning disabilities received their instruction in self-contained classrooms, the most restrictive environments, for more than 50% of the instructional day. In essence, these special education classrooms had become "schools within schools" (Shapiro, 1993), where special education students were segregated from the general education population, which included the majority of Anglo students.

To decrease the large numbers of students receiving instruction in the most restrictive environments, Sunshine ISD began to consider inclusionary practices as a means to move students into less restrictive educational settings. At the same time that this school district was considering inclusion, I began working on my doctorate in educational leadership. At this time, I decided that I would become a change agent by helping transform the ways that the district delivered its special education services to students. I felt strongly that special education was a service, not a location, and I was determined that mindsets could be changed regarding dumping students in special education classrooms for long periods of time when they qualified as having exceptional conditions. I engaged in serious reflection regarding the inclusion of special education students at the two small elementary schools to which I was assigned. Many students with learning disabilities had learning needs that were substantially different from non-disabled students. Could these academic and social needs best be met in general education settings? Could these students receive an appropriate education when they were totally mainstreamed? Could their IEPs best be implemented in the general education classroom? Would inclusionary practices cause an overload on general education teachers who were already stressed by the challenges of high-stakes testing? Would higher students become tutors to them at the expense of their own academic growth? These were some of my considerations regarding inclusion.

BECOMING A CHANGE AGENT FOR INCLUSION

In becoming a change agent regarding inclusionary practices, I first considered the resources available to my school. Fortunately, my school was located in a university town, and the Department of Special Education could provide some important assistance in the process of inclusion. The university was implementing a large grant that funded the research on the implementation of a direct instruction reading and math program. Many practicum students were participating in this study, and they needed a setting where they could implement this direct instructional reading and math program. In addition, I discovered that the Educational Service Center (ESC) for our region was funding some minigrants to facilitate inclusion. I talked to the principal at Pineland Elementary about the possibility of collaborating with the local university on a direct instruction reading program, which I felt would reduce the number of referrals to special education. I also discussed the possibility of applying for an inclusion grant through the ESC to obtain funds for staff development and educational materials, which would help increase the success of inclusionary practices.

Ms. Carson was the principal of Pineland Elementary School, and she wholeheartedly believed in the principles of inclusion. The majority of her school was culturally diverse, and she greatly valued multicultural education. Ms. Carson was the kind of administrator who struggled with the expectations of central administrators for her to control her schools' operations in such a manner that they produced the kind of workers that society values in the most efficient and economically feasible manner as possible. Instead, she attempted to create an educational environment where learning communities flourished, challenging the assumptions of accountability and standardization. She confronted the fact that many of the school district's structures and practices did not reflect many of the values espoused by education that related to care and respect for persons and to opportunities for growth and development. As an educational leader, Ms. Carson was committed to an ethical stance that supported a multicultural community of continual learners. This leader was very aware of the ways that schools subtract resources, such as cultural identities, languages, and cultural identities, from students by the process of cultural assimilation, content and organization of curriculum, and teachers' biased, noncaring pedagogy, attitudes, and actions (Valenzuela, 1999). She firmly believed that schools should make their curriculum "challenging and supportive" to students in order to help them stay on a path to achieving their fullest academic potentials.

As an educational leader, Ms. Carson focused on centering students' learning on a moral ethic of caring that nurtured and valued relationships. She valued expressive discourse that demonstrated regard for human affections and feelings based on situational contexts. Ms. Carson's pedagogy of caring encompassed a value of students' diverse cultures and languages as well as multicultural curriculum, true bilingual education, relevant learning activities, high standards of achievement, expressive discourse, cooperation and socialization, and freedom of students' voices (Valenzuela, 1999). She advocated that teachers embrace an authentic caring ideology and practice. Teachers and students were to connect in sincere trusting relationships built on respect, and these relationships would be the foundation of all learning. Ms. Carson encouraged teachers to become more informed regarding their students' various cultures. In addition, they needed to engage in continual critical reflection regarding their pedagogical practice until they resolved issues that were hindering students from attaining their fullest potentials while maintaining the richness of students' cultural diversity.

At teacher-assistance team meetings, Ms. Carson demanded more effective interventions as prereferral strategies in general education classrooms. She supported students' referrals to special education as a last resort. Ms. Carson had expressed concern to me regarding the district's emphasis on the quantity of material covered at the expense of reteaching concepts to students who did not acquire important concepts the first time the material was presented; the school district supported the practice of teachers covering as much grade-level material as possible to prepare students for high-stakes testing. Since many students were below grade level, they were not successful with grade-level instructional activities and materials, and many required reteaching that slowed down the process of accountability, the process of preparation for high-stakes testing. I provided Ms. Carson with some articles on the efficacy of direct instruction with students of lower socioeconomic status, and she became interested in obtaining some direct instructional materials and some additional staff who could implement a direct instructional reading program. The stage was set for a partnership with the grant team at the local university and an application for an inclusion grant through the Educational Region Center.

During spring break, Ms. Carson and I assembled an inclusion team of general education and special education teachers to work on plans for applying for the Inclusion Project Grant through the Educational Service Center. The goal of the grant was to provide inclusive assistance in general education settings so that students would become risk takers, attempt more difficult tasks, participate more in cooperative group classroom activities, develop higher critical and creative thinking skills, have more opportunities to engage socially with their grade-appropriate, nondisabled peers, and experience a variety of learning experiences in the least restrictive environment. In essence, this project would enable these students to obtain their fullest intellectual, academic, social, emotional, and physical potentials.

As a community of learners, our staff, including special education and general education teachers, would work collaboratively as a team designing and implementing differentiating curriculum and instruction in order to accommodate all learners' individual needs. Special education teachers would participate in grade-level meetings held once each week to discuss curriculum and instruction, and a special education teacher would serve on the school's Campus Advisory Council to assist in writing campus goals, objectives, and strategies for the 2004–2005 school year.

In April of 2003, we submitted our grant, and in the following May, we were notified that we received the grant along with five other schools in the East Texas region. Although the monetary allocation for the grant was only $5,000, this financial support would enable the staff at Pineland Elementary to have access to important staff development opportunities and needed instructional materials. In addition, the Title I reading program at the school would utilize six highly trained university practicum students who would teach at-risk students basic reading skills using a direct instruction program in a general education setting on a daily basis. These at-risk students would likely be referred to special education sometime during the academic year if Title I assistance and instructional accommodations were not sufficient in increasing their reading skills.

By participating in the ESC Inclusion Project, Pineland Elementary succeeded in expanding a co-teach model in order to provide inclusive assistance to as many students as possible so that they became risk takers, attempted more difficult tasks, participated more in classroom activities, interacted socially in an appropriate manner with others, and experienced a variety of learning experiences in the least restrictive environment. In addition, students were instructed in the "hidden curriculum" of the school; they were provided with tours of the school, peer guidance, and teacher assistance. With assistance of the grant, an effective model of direct instruction for reading was implemented for general education and special education students in a general education setting. This systematic instruction model provided specific instructional materials and highly organized systematic methods of teaching, motivating students, managing the classroom, and assessing student progress. Pineland Elementary School's participation in the Inclusion Project provided quality educational experiences in the least restrictive environment so that students could increase their decision making, build higher-order thinking skills, and take ownership in analyzing the content of their studies. All teachers received training in meeting each learner's individual needs by differentiating content, process, product, and learning environment according to the student's readiness, interests, and learning profile through a range of instructional and management strategies, such as multiple intelligences, varied questioning strategies, graphic organizers, interest centers, and independent study (Tomlinson, 1999). All students were provided with high-quality instruction in the least restrictive setting so that they would experience educational success and develop to their fullest intellectual, academic, social, emotional, and physical potentials.

The benefits of Pineland Elementary's participation in the Inclusion Project Grant were astounding. First, special needs students began to feel that they were members of communities of learning within general education classrooms. As a result of inclusionary activities, these students developed more appropriate social skills and increased self-esteem. In addition, these students had access to grade-level curriculum and high expectations. Through the grant, a co-teach model of instruction was implemented. This model encompassed special education and general education teachers taking turns providing academic instruction to students in general education settings. Through this model of instructional delivery, special education teachers' expectations of students' academic achievement increased, and these teachers acquired knowledge of grade-level curriculum standards. At the same time, general education teachers learned special instructional strategies that were effective with all students by observing special education teachers' instructional activities. At-risk students who were provided direct instruction in reading by the practicum students in a general education setting made significant gains in reading, and as a result of this achievement, there were fewer referrals to special education.

The continuing goal of Pineland Elementary is for all students to be accountable for their learning, to be independent and responsible citizens, to appreciate diversity, to possess strong work ethics, and to acquire a love for learning. At Pineland Elementary, we continue on our journey toward equitable instruction. At the present time, we have only one student who receives instruction in the special education setting for most of the day, and we plan to implement more inclusionary activities with this student next year. This year, all students receiving special education passed the state-mandated competency tests in reading, writing, and math, and the school's overall scores on these tests increased so much that the school achieved a recognized status, very close to an exemplary one. General education and special education students benefited from higher-quality instruction than they had in the past as a result of the Inclusion Project.

FUTURE PLANS FOR INCLUSION

Next year, we will expand the Inclusion Project at Pineland Elementary. Recently, the school was awarded another Inclusion Project Grant by the Education Service Center. In addition to the $5,000 allocated for this grant, Pineland Elementary was awarded an additional $3,000 for implementing the previous grant in an exceptional manner. During the next academic year, we plan for more special education students to take grade-level, state-mandated competency tests (the Texas Assessment of Knowledge and Skills), instead of alternative state tests that are available to special education students (the State Developed Alternative Assessment), as they have increased opportunities to grade-level curriculum in general education settings. We also want to expand differentiated instruction within general education settings so that special education students will have access to grade-level curriculum and high expectations.

At Pineland Elementary, we continue on our journey toward equitable instruction. As an educational leader, I have succeeded in promoting human welfare, justice, and fairness; which are elements of my moral philosophy, by participating in the inclusion grant. My decision to facilitate the implementation of inclusionary practices at Pineland Elementary was supported by good reasons, and at the same time, I considered each individual's interest.

I had no idea how much my life would change as I continued my journey down the road to learning as a cohort member in a doctoral program. My increased awareness of social justice issues and equity in education served as the impetus for my involvement in the inclusion grants at Pineland Elementary.

During the last year, my moral philosophy has truly grown in relation to issues of tracking and inclusion that I have encountered as an educational diagnostician in a small East Texas rural school district. I continue to strive for a systematic understanding of the nature of morality and what it requires of me as an educational leader, and I continue to try to bridge the gap between theory and practice as a scholar-practitioner leader. I realize that quick fixes to improving student test scores, such as tracking and placement in special education settings, are insufficient and morally unjust. I also realize that the ends of high test scores do not justify the means of treating students inequitably, denying them equal access to instructional opportunities, grade-level curriculum, and social interaction with their same-age/grade peers. I will continue to be a change agent in a community of moral concern as I strive for all students to have access to differentiated instruction based on their learning styles, strengths, and challenges, as well as appropriate, challenging curriculum, so that they will attain their fullest academic, intellectual, social/emotional, and physical potentials.

Sharon Kathleen Ninness is an educational diagnostician and an adjunct instructor for Stephen F. Austin State University.

CHOOSING TO CHANGE

Terri R. Hebert

> Where the old tracks are lost, new country is revealed with its wonder.
>
> —Rabindranath Tagore (Cook, 1997, p. 300)

Imagine standing on a very high peak in the Rocky Mountains, at a special place called the Continental Divide. The air has thinned due to the extreme altitude. The sky is a crisp blue with tiny wisps of clouds breathtakingly close, bidding you to stretch your arm out and feel the vapor.

Imagine that you are a single raindrop falling upon that special place. As you fall and hit the ground, you are split into two water droplets . . . one falling toward the west and one falling toward the east. One will ultimately lead toward the Pacific Ocean and one toward the Atlantic. A destiny has been forever altered; a direction has completely changed.

Unlike a raindrop, which is nonliving and inanimate, educators are faced with a multitude of choices throughout their careers. Many times, we are oblivious to the impact of our decisions, being required to make them with so little time to analyze and interpret possible outcomes. Within a science classroom, students learn to expect and even appreciate change as they are taught to discover the cause-and-effect relationship.

Reflecting upon life, one might observe a single decision that forever impacted his or her practice and the future. For a transformational educator, that moment often revolves around a choice to move away from the commonality of the crowd and begin a journey down a path seldom trod. This walk takes the individual into an unknown world, and the twists and turns are sometimes perilous and frightening. The passionate strength for this journey is found within the soul and enables one to persevere until the task has been completed.

LEADING OR BEING LED

As a newly hired science administrator in a midsized school district, I was overwhelmed by the enormous amount of work to be done. There was not much time for reflection or for building relationships. I found myself working 10-hour days, rarely getting up from behind my desk. I believed success required sacrifice, and I definitely wanted to achieve in my job, so I obediently did what I was told without questions or without time to reflect. During the first month, I was asked to introduce a new secondary science curriculum to the teachers. The atmosphere was not accepting or trusting of this new curriculum, or of a new science coordinator. The instructors wanted to know why and how, and I found myself bombarded on all sides by anger and confusion. Even the principals were questioning the need to focus on science, when reading, language arts, and mathematics were the content areas tested. I found myself out on a limb, completely alone, with little training involving conflict or crowd control.

Change is never easy, and the struggle that ensued continued throughout the first year. Then I found myself really beginning to listen to the teachers as they expressed their ideas and opinions of science education. Toward the end of the second year, I began to observe a change occurring among the community as trust and cooperation began to grow, facilitating the development of a vertical team approach to science, and hope began to emerge for all stakeholders. Despite this new growth, I began to closely examine my foundational beliefs about education and about science, and I found no substantial answers. My inner self was troubled by what I had seen and by my willingness to follow without anticipating the impact of my actions. Why was there such a resistance to change? Why was there a lack of trust among educators? Why were new ideas not valued, as well as people?

Even though the new science program had begun to make some progress, in March of the second year I was told that the district would be reducing the number of administrators at the conclusion of the school term; my position would be one of the 18 included in the reduction. I would no longer have a job as of July. Feelings of confusion and anger flooded my soul, but the most intense emotion was that of grief. How could this happen to me? I had worked long hours and complied with the instructions of my supervisor. I was even seeing growth and change occur among our teachers. The state and nation were clearly communicating the necessity of scientifically literate citizens, yet the district did not see the need for my position. My idea of success came crumbling in around me. I had given my all to assist in the process of change, but I found it ending as quickly as it had begun.

Reflecting back on this time in my life, I now realize that this was my Continental Divide. I faced a decision of monumental proportions that would forever change my destiny. I could go back into the classroom, or I could accept a university position as a teacher-in-residence. Returning as a classroom teacher would resemble someone coming home after a treacherous journey. It was a safe and comfortable environment for me, and I believed that I could make a positive difference in the lives of my future students. To be honest, I was tempted to accept the position of seventh-grade science teacher within the district. However, my difficulty in choosing was based on the fact that I now realized that my idea of science education did not align with the district's idea of education.

My second choice, to become a teacher-in-residence, involved working with a small group of university personnel as they sought to establish a new mathematics and science program dedicated to teacher training. In conjunction with my transcontinental divide of career choices, I received notification of being accepted into an educational leadership doctoral program. These new options seemed to be risky and involved unknown territories, but they also promised to engage me in multiple opportunities possibly leading toward growth and change. My decision to enter the university environment, as well as the doctoral program, became my raindrop's point of contact, and my journey toward the ocean began.

THE DAWNING OF A NEW DAY

Only a few weeks earlier, I felt as if my future had disintegrated around me. Now, excitement and anticipation were racing through my veins. I felt alive once more with the promise of a new journey. The sun's appearance signaled the start of another East Texas summer day, and it promised to fulfill the weatherman's forecast of hot and sticky. As I drove toward the university to begin the doctoral program, my mind reflected upon the day I entered into the first grade. I remembered the feelings of excitement, coupled with a nervous anticipation of what to expect. Even now, I could still see the image of my teacher, standing at the door to welcome each new student. Everything appeared to be huge: the desks, the chairs, and the room.

As I entered into the classroom on the fourth floor of the education building, I also felt very small. I was a new student unfamiliar with the campus, and the professors appeared larger than life. I realized after brief introductions that I was among a group of intelligent and capable individuals. I questioned how and why I came to be a part of this group. Did I have what it must take to endure the enormous workload? Did I really want to change? What did the term "cohort" mean anyway? The drive home provided me with some quiet time, and I reflected upon the words of wisdom and the cautionary advice that had been given by students farther along in the program. Sleep did not come easily that night. I remember dreaming that someone had placed a hat upon my head, and an ever-increasing suction was forming around the brim. The force became so tight that it was impossible to remove the hat. My head hurt and my brains felt as if they were going to be stretched beyond normal boundaries! As I awakened the next morning and shared my dream with a friend, we viewed this as a prophetic experience, unveiling a momentary glimpse of what was to come.

During the course of that first summer, my raindrop's speed accelerated as it rushed downward through the high ridges and crevices found along the mountain face. My thoughts and beliefs were being challenged at incredible speeds, and often I merely hung on while the course proceeded. Battles raged within me as I was forced to deal with personal and spiritual issues.

Parker Palmer (1990) discusses a moment in his life where he was participating in an Outward Bound program. During an afternoon's activity, he was asked to walk down the face of a cliff. Unable to see the course that was before him, and completely entrusting his life to the harness system and the instructors, he attached himself to the gossamer strand and flung his feet away from the ground and into the unknown. As he progressed downward, he found himself entering into a very large hole in the rock. Fear overtook him and he froze. He was unable to move to the right or left, and only with the gentle encouraging of his instructor was he able to continue. Then, as he hung there in an almost lifeless state, someone called to him, "If you can't get out of it, get into it" (p. 33). As I found myself during that first semester of my doctoral studies facing a very large hole of doubt and confusion, I was also frozen. I did not know how to continue on this journey, or even if I could. I also faced a similar choice. I could remove myself from the program and return to life as it was before, or I could commit myself to move ahead towards the hole and learn how to successfully maneuver until I reached the other side. I chose to go deeper and remain active throughout the process of change.

Margaret Wheatley (1999) wrote, "Belief is the place from which true change originates" (p. 3). For true change to occur within each individual, we had to travel to a place hidden to outsiders. We ventured into our inner depths with fearful trepidation as we were asked to examine foundational beliefs. This proved to be a very difficult task. We examined antiquities that were corroded with rust, and as we deconstructed them, we found that they stubbornly held their ground. After a fierce battle, the structure came crashing down around us. We erected new structures, new thoughts and beliefs, only to have them falter under the weight of closer examination. Wheatley (1999) echoed our change process by asserting, "In this world of things, change is not motion, but a description of a new state. . . . Rather than understanding change as continuous, creative energy, it becomes nothing but a redesign" (p. 93).

A PARADIGM SHIFT

As an administrator, I had held the belief that I was completely responsible for all science-related tasks, including professional development, student achievement, and curriculum creation and alignment. I was moving in isolation, instead of in harmony with my co-workers. I had missed many valuable opportunities to collaborate with teachers, parents, and community members, and this did not allow them an active role in the development of the district's science education program.

A doctoral class assignment was to read Gordon Donaldson's book *Cultivating Leadership in Schools: Connecting People, Purpose, and Practice*. After the first few paragraphs, I found my reading pace quickening. It was as if I had not been fed in a very long time. I could not get enough of the words, and I quickly gobbled them up. The digestion process of the ideas found within the pages was a different matter. It was a much slower process, and I found myself struggling with my prior beliefs about control. Who actually controlled a school district? Was it the administrators, or was it the faculty? Could it possibly be the parents? Was control actually required to manage the faculty and staff on a campus or within a district? The administrators who had served as my role models understood the necessity of control and masterfully utilized the skill in the decision-making process.

Where did I fall on the continuum of control? As I reflected upon that visual image, I thought back to my disastrous introduction of the secondary science curriculum. Had I valued the input of the faculty and staff, I would have sought out their comments and their questions privately. Instead, in an effort to control this change, I had passed out the curriculum to the masses during an in-service meeting without any forewarning or any type of preparation. I fully expected them to openly accept the document since it originated from the central office, and at the same time, I desired their acceptance of me and the deceptive authority that my title carried with it. Due to the crowd's negative response, I counteracted in a destructive manner as the harshness of their comments continued to lash out at my ego. In the privacy of my office, I broke down weeping and found myself confused and even fearful of having to face the teachers again. Had I understood how leadership can facilitate change and had I known the value of collaboration and collegiality in that process, my delivery of the curriculum would have changed, saving me weeks and months of agony and unnecessary battles.

Donaldson's (2001) words seem to be directed to me alone as he clearly pointed out that "leadership cannot be exercised alone" (p. 146). He mentioned that a true leader finds unique ways of merging key stakeholders' talents, dreams, and purposes into something new and uniquely designed to support student learning. Donaldson (2001) closed his book by stating, "We can each help to propel our schools forward if we choose honest relationships, child-centered purposes, and a commitment to act in concert. We can all be leaders if we choose" (p. 153).

My raindrop had settled in a quiet pool as I reflected upon this profound notion of change. I found myself slowly, but clearly understanding how all community members—whether it is the school community, the neighborhood, or the family—are responsible in the education of a child, not only those with administrative titles. I longed for an opportunity to return to my previous job and redo all that had been done. But I also knew that had I remained, I might have never experienced this pivotal moment of understanding.

INVOLVED IN THE ACT OF BECOMING

This changing concept of leadership transformed my approach to education and opened new avenues from which to explore. Today, the empowerment of teamwork at the university has provided my colleagues and me opportunities to grow and change as we each explore our changing potential. The strength and courage required as we move through the change process is nothing less than extraordinary. Duffy (2003) identified this when he pointed out that redesigning a system, whether it is found within a school setting or a human being, is a daunting task requiring a special kind of leader. In fact, "Being courageous does not mean being without fear. Being courageous means facing fear and doing what has to be done in spite of it" (p. 5).

My journey as a raindrop has been a speedy one, as I have encountered many new and interesting places throughout the first year of the doctoral program. It is difficult for me to imagine myself at the journey's conclusion, knowing that there will still be many skirmishes fought along the battleground of understanding. There is still much to learn, to experience, and to observe. I anticipate the classes ahead and wonder what they will require of me. As each semester ends and a new one starts, I feel a growing sense of accomplishment within me. I have learned to enjoy the battles that wage war upon my soul for it is within these battles that I truly come to understand my rationale for the decisions I make. In this same way, I have obtained a clearer understanding for the need to embrace change and all that accompanies this process. I understand that we are often asked to let go of our outdated perspectives and our old systems. Letting go is often hard, but it is in that moment that we experience a true sense of freedom. It is as if our raindrop, after its long and treacherous journey, has come to the place where multitudes of other raindrops are waiting to welcome it home. One day, I will also experience such a peace, but for now, I am content to travel along in this journey of growth in search of becoming.

Terri R. Hebert is currently teacher-in-residence for the Teaching Excellence in Mathematics and Science Program at the University of Texas at Tyler.

OUT OF CULTURAL BONDAGE INTO THE PROMISED LAND OF CULTURAL DIVERSITY

Paul Vickers

> And the Lord said, "I have surely seen the oppression of My people in Egypt, and have heard their cry because of their taskmasters, for I know their sorrows. So I have come down to deliver them out of the hand of the Egyptians, and to bring them up from that land, to a land flowing with milk and honey."
>
> —Exodus 3:7–8

I walked into the first class as a doctoral cohort member feeling an incredible sense of anxiety. I had a variety of doubts and uncertainties, which seemed to shout internally, "I'm not talented enough or able enough for a program like this. I don't know if I will have time for this. These people must be much more intelligent than I. My experiences are so limited." I truly felt inadequate for the task.

My concerns, however, were not strong enough to keep me from continuing the program. Today, four semesters later, I am so glad that I did not give up. The relationships with students and professors, the educational knowledge I have gained, and the spiritual growth I have experienced are profound.

On this journey, the knowledge that I have gained has led me to a greater understanding of educational theory and practice, but this learning has also done much more for me personally through my growth as a spiritual person. I am just beginning to recognize the true needs of those around me. I am learning to appreciate other cultures, not only in my educational practice as a principal but also throughout life in general.

WAYS THAT I USED TO LEAD

Before I began the doctoral program and gained experience as a school administrator, I was limited in recognizing the needs of others. In my first administrative role as an assistant principal at a small rural high school, I wanted to make a good impression. I also wanted to be known as a strong disciplinarian. Once, a teacher came to me complaining about a student who did nothing but sleep in her classroom. I asked her if she had spoken with him about it, and she said that she had on several occasions. The teacher, and several other teachers, told me that the student was a constant problem in class.

I did what I thought any good administrator would do. I called him to my office and gave him morning detention. The detention supervisor came to my office the next morning and told me that the student had slept in detention. I called the student back in and informed him that he would be in our in-school suspension program for the next few days for failure to follow the rules of detention.

Late that afternoon, a middle-aged Hispanic mother came to my office. In very broken English, she informed me that she was the student's mother. She told me that the student had to work late in the evening at a chicken processing plant to help support them. She also told me that he had difficulty understanding his teachers due to the language barrier. Wanting to set the tone as a "tough administrator," I informed the mother that school needed to be more important to him, that he needed to try harder, and that he would have to obey the rules. I'll never forget the defeated look of that mother when she left my office. Today, I reflect back on this event with deep regret.

Being from a background that could be characterized as "closed minded," I found the idea of learning from different experiences, philosophies, and ideas foreign, but the new ideas and philosophies I've been exposed to in the doctoral program have helped me to open myself to new and, sometimes, uncomfortable ground. Today, I am becoming a much more spiritually reflective person, and I am much quicker to learn than to judge. I had always considered myself to be an open-minded person to society and culture as a whole, but now I see just how culture and social status can affect our treatment and opinions of other societies and cultures.

THE NEW WAY I LEAD

Recently, I faced another experience involving a student who did not qualify for a select organization. I investigated the matter and found that the decision makers had followed proper procedures for selection. They had done everything right as stated in the policy book. However, I had difficulty with the reasons for not allowing the student into the organization. The honor roll student had overcome a great deal of adversity in his young life. The decision makers felt that the student did not exhibit the "personal qualities" for the organization.

I visited with one of my mentors in the administrative field. Because he was a doctoral student himself, I shared with him my misgivings about the whole scenario. He shared with me a bit of profound wisdom that I still try to use when facing questions related to social justice and equity. He said, "It sounds like you and the committee did what was right, but did you do the right thing?" Becoming more reflective in my practice, I have learned to dig deeper before making judgments.

Being in a doctoral program has truly been a spiritual journey for me, full of experiences that have led me through many triumphs and travails. On a much, much smaller scale, I characterize my journey with Moses in the Old Testament of the Bible as he was faced with the challenge of leading the Hebrews to the Promised Land. Along Moses' journey he not only discovered many things about God, the Hebrew people, and the journey, but also about himself. I find that on this journey I am truly discovering a great deal not only about authors, ideas, and concepts but also about myself and how I perceive and treat others from different cultures.

I CAN'T SPEAK

As Moses had his revelatory experience from God in the form of the "bush that was not consumed by the fire," he felt his own inadequacy. When God presented him with the task, he presented his excuses. He indicated that he was not the man for the job. God insisted. He rationalized that his inability to speak would hinder him. God insisted. He pleaded that he could not do it. God insisted. His feelings of inadequacy could not hinder his destiny.

My own feelings of inadequacy brought a great deal of doubt. I did not know if I belonged in the doctoral program. On the drive home the afternoon of the first day, and frankly for the first month, I wondered if I was the only one who needed a dictionary (an expanded dictionary) to understand what the professors were saying; I certainly was not. Over time, Moses' faith in God provided the confidence he needed. Over time, the confidence I've gained in my own abilities as a scholar and practitioner have improved.

Many of my former doubts and fears can be traced back to a personal cultural bondage shaped by limited cultural experiences. I came from a rural, middle-class, white family who had, for the most part, limited educational and cultural experiences. Though some in my family attended college, I am the only one in my immediate and extended family who holds a college degree. Due to very limited income, most of my family has never been to a foreign country (including myself). This, among other limitations, caused me to feel inadequate in comparison to many of my educational peers.

My confidence has often been shaped by my self-perception, and not necessarily the opinions of others. While God believed in Moses, Moses did not believe in Moses. While my peers and professors may have expressed confidence in my abilities, I did not believe in myself. I was afraid to move away from the culture that bound me. The words of Duffy (2003) encouraged me: "Being courageous does not mean being without fear. Being courageous means facing fear and doing what has to be done in spite of it" (p. 5). Duffy describes that *unwavering courage* comes by consistently facing fear with courage. As I faced my fears in becoming an instructional leader, I knew that I needed to be confident toward working on a doctorate degree.

LET MY PEOPLE GO

When Moses set his sights on freeing the Hebrews (his own people), he found that he had to convince a stubborn, stiff-necked, dominant force in the man Pharaoh for this to happen. He had to not only have the courage to convince Pharaoh, but also have the courage to convince the Hebrew people of this. He had to not only use the power given to him, but have the courage to use this power in a positive way. He had to have the courage to stand before Pharaoh and say, "My people have been oppressed long enough. Let my people go!"

One of the greatest lessons that I have learned from my doctoral classes deals with my influence and the influence of others regarding culture. As a school administrator, I have influence on a daily basis over students. My actions and words can oppress or enlighten. They can wound or encourage. I have made it my mission to also convince the teaching and support staff of this. It takes a great deal of courage to stand against oppression.

How school programs impact students of different racial, gender, and class backgrounds has become very important to me through my growth in the doctoral program. Those who have perpetually been without power or voice (in this case, the students) often accept programmatic school changes because those in power desire the changes. Freire (1993) pointed out that the oppressed adapt to the structure of domination that they have lived in. He indicates that they accept it and become resigned to it. They are inhibited from waging the struggle for freedom as long as they feel incapable of running the risks the struggle requires.

In schools, students often blindly accept their fate. The school leader must have the courage to stand against inequities in teaching and schooling, and stand in the gap for students. The school leader must adhere to this challenge even when oppressed students don't realize that they are being oppressed. Moses stood in the gap for a people who didn't understand God's plan revealed to Moses. School leaders must understand that their roles are to guide the structure and plan of schools to incorporate and collaborate with all voices.

In working with the cohort model in our particular doctoral program, I have gained experience in the power of community. Understanding that it is imperative to hear the voices of all has become a practical experience within our cohort. This variety of cultures has merged into a community of learners with power in the process.

ON MOUNT SINAI

After the great miracles of the parting of the Red Sea and the water that flowed from the rock (representing God's care for the people), the Hebrews finally reached Mount Sinai. Moses went up the mountain to receive the commandments and laws from God. I'm sure he experienced some wonderful things on that mountain. As he was learning the commandments and laws himself, I'm also sure he could not begin to foresee the ramifications that they would bring.

What an incredible experience being on the mountain, yet in contrast, it must have been frustrating to come down, with the Ten Commandments written by God in hand, to see that the people had no idea of what had been happening on the mountain. Seeing them dancing around a golden calf, Moses became so frustrated that he shattered the Ten Commandments. Going back up the mountain, he would have to "chisel out" the commandments by his own hand.

While I have gained much by being in a doctoral program, I have had to "chisel out" my own understanding of theory and how it relates to practice. Much of the knowledge I am still trying to digest. I am learning what it is to truly be a scholar and a practitioner. Jenlink (2001) suggests, "The ideal of scholar-practitioner leadership envisions a 'new scholarship' wherein the practitioner as a scholar of practice seeks to mediate professional practice and formal knowledge and theory through disciplined inquiry, and uses scholarly inquiry and practice to guide decisions on all levels of educational activity" (p. 7). The world of the scholar-practitioner encompasses a variety of ideas and philosophies. It is concerned with questions of emancipation. It grapples with purpose and meaning not only in theory but also in practice. Kincheloe and Steinberg (1999) allude to human dignity, freedom, authority, and responsibility as a role of the researcher and the practitioner. In an effort to chisel out my own understanding of theory and how it relates to practice, I keep in mind Murphy's (1992) admonition that the "construction of knowledge should move to the foreground, the dissemination of information to the background" (p. 144). This is a critical role of the doctoral program.

One of the most frustrating aspects of being a school leader in a doctoral program is that I come to the mountain every other weekend and discuss theory and practice, I learn and experience such valuable knowledge, and then I come down to a place where other colleagues often do not understand. I want to create a socially just, caring, courageous, moral, and democratic society in my school, but many of those around me don't always hear what I'm saying.

Schools need to be places that shun oppressive practices and should, instead, seek to embrace diversity and social justice. In my search for greater understanding, I have found that I need to lead our school community in developing a school culture of caring and understanding where policies and practices keep learners at the heart of practice. Donaldson's (2001) definition of leadership resonates for me: "Leadership can be said to exist in a school only insofar as it contributes demonstrably to growing, healthy, skilled, and well-adjusted children" (p. 43). This could be characterized as keeping learners at the heart of practice.

I recently had a conference with a teacher concerning a student in her class who was struggling academically. I wondered why this particular student was thriving in his other classes, but not in this teacher's class. The teacher informed me that she felt the student was doing fine under the circumstances. I asked, "What circumstances do you mean?" The teacher shared that the student had no home life and came from a different background than many of the other students in our school. The teacher also indicated that I should not worry because the student would probably squeak by with a C.

As I reflected more and more on this conversation, I became convinced that this student's problem was that the teacher had reduced expectations for the student. The student "squeaked by" because it was all that the teacher expected. Too often, educators in their sympathy for a student's circumstances have good intentions, but they do not keep the student's best interest at heart. Instead of taking students to the mountaintop, we take them to the top of an anthill. When we limit our students' mountaintop experiences, we limit our own.

WANDERING IN THE WILDERNESS

The Hebrews lack of courage to go into the Promised Land and the desire to go back to the land of oppression caused them to wander in the desert for 40 years. There was a courageous leader named Caleb who declared, "We should go and take possession of the land for we can certainly do it." The Hebrews failed to hear him for fear of the risks involved. Freire (1998) refers to this as a "fear of freedom."

Before entering the doctoral program, I truly thought of myself as culturally diverse and socially just. I have many minority friends and acquaintances. I am charitable when it comes to giving to the economically disadvantaged. I never realized that in being ever supportive of the dominant culture of my school, without seeking to understand and relate to other cultures than my own, that I was actually supporting the status quo of the dominant culture. It is important that teaching be seen as affecting all students from every cultural and social stratum.

School leaders must be courageous enough to stand up and say, "Together, we can do this! Together, we can create communities where all can learn. Together, we can create a culture of change." I say "together" because it will take belief in a common vision to see change in a school. Caleb did not go alone. He knew the people would have to get behind the change and overcome their fears. Fullan (2001) challenged, "The litmus test of all leadership is whether it mobilizes people's commitment to putting their energy into actions designed to improve things. It is individual commitment, but it is above all collective mobilization" (p. 9). I believe that it will take this in education in order to escape the wilderness within education.

THE PROMISED LAND

It is interesting to note that Moses was never allowed to cross the Jordan and enter into the Promised Land. Suffice it to say, his attitude and action got the best of him. However, God did allow Moses to get a glimpse of the Promised Land before he died.

Within the realm of understanding that I've been exposed to concerning education and life, maybe the most important thing is to provide ourselves with glimpses of the Promised Land. We are in a permanent state of searching for the Promised Land. We are ever learning and ever growing in our relationships with our peers and our students. We hope to catch glimpses of the Promised Land, and unfortunately, on occasion we slip back into the wilderness. I have found that we are, in the words of Freire, (2001), *unfinished*. This *unfinishedness* is essential to our human condition. We live, and, therefore, we are unfinished. Freire states, "The experience of openness as a founding moment of our unfinishedness leads us to knowledge and unawareness of that unfinishedness" (p. 121).

As I entered the doctoral program, I honestly felt that if I could survive the program I would be complete. I would have nowhere else to go. I would become the authority. Now I know that even when I complete the program, I will still be *unfinished*, incomplete as I continue on my journey. My views of culture, caring, knowledge, learning, teaching, and democracy have all been challenged. I realize that the struggle is really the most critical. As Moses struggled to fulfill his mission and to catch a glimpse of the Promised Land, so will I.

I recently was hired to be a principal of an elementary campus with a growing Hispanic population. One of the new challenges that I will face is helping our staff work together to chisel out a vision that encompasses all learners. We will not only have to become sensitive to the learning strategies of our students but also to the hearts of our students.

During my first days on the job, a young, Hispanic girl (probably a first grader) ran up to me and hugged my leg so tightly that there was no escaping her. Someone had obviously told her that I was to be her new principal. She was in summer school to gain support in reading. Her English was very limited. I stooped down to be eye level with her and asked if she was excited about school. Her eyes sparkled as she told me (in very broken English) about all of the things she was learning in school. She hugged me around the neck and went back to her class. I entered my office with tears in my eyes. I had seen a glimpse of the Promise Land. My mission and ministry had been set before me. My "commandment" was clear: lead children to the Promised Land.

Paul Vickers is currently the principal of David Crockett Elementary School in Marshall, Texas.

UNLOCKING THE GATES: ENTERING THE REALM OF UNDERSTANDING

Sherry Durham

He who opens a school door, closes a prison.

—Victor Hugo (1862)

THE GATEKEEPER

Each day I unlock five gates that allow access to our campus for 659 of our 815 students. These are children who step into the dark morning while most of us are still sleeping to await the school bus that will carry them to school and, later in the day, home again. For the most part, these are children with parents who work the night shift or who leave before daylight for their jobs. These are children of poverty. Most are on free or reduced lunch. Many of these children never have parents show up for teacher conferences, nor are their parents in the audience at school programs. These are children with worn-out shoes and too-tight jackets they refuse to remove even as the day grows warmer. These are also the children who wait patiently for me to find my keys to the gates while I search my pockets, if I have been delayed for a few minutes. These are the children, the same children, who wave and smile from the window of the school bus each afternoon as

I lock the gates against any intruders who may attempt to enter the campus in the darkness of night.

All of these children come to school to learn and I hold the keys in my hand that will enable this process to occur. As an assistant principal, I am an educational leader and it is my charge to invite all children to join in the learning experience of gaining a quality education. To do this, I must be able to transform my campus into a place where all children feel welcome and secure to engage in the processes and strategies of learning. I must become an invitational leader empowering teachers, paraprofessionals, custodians, and cafeteria workers to create a community that evokes a shared commitment to inviting all children to the table of education and ensuring that none are left out because of their socioeconomic status or ethnicity.

NEW VISION

There was a time in my practice when I did not see the whole child. These children represented numbers in my head, numbers of low socioeconomic, Hispanic, and African American children. Often these children present the ultimate challenge to a campus attempting to reach 90% passing rates in reading, writing, and math on the Texas Assessment of Knowledge and Skills (TAKS) test in all subgroups as mandated by the state of Texas. On an elementary campus in Texas, there is a danger of relegating children into two groups: those who master objectives on the state-mandated accountability test (TAKS) and those who do not. Unfortunately, too often, many of those sleepy faces in the hazy morning light fall into the "do not" category.

My strength is curriculum alignment. I have spent 10 years working on strategies and remediation programs to bring children closer to passing the state assessment for progress required by the state of Texas. I always viewed myself as a caring person with a true concern for all children to reach their potential and the high expectations the educational system had in place for them. Accountability is a good thing. It provides goals and data that will enable instruction to become closely aligned with expectation. Information gathered from testing in the classroom and through regularly administered benchmarks provides a clear picture of instructional needs and strengths that can guide curriculum implementation. This is also where the dividing line is drawn for those who will need after-school tutorials or extended time in summer programs. But as I pointed out, in the educational administrator business, often just the numbers, equaling 90%—that is all I need to have a successful campus and enhance my career standing in the sight of my superiors.

Then, I entered a doctoral program and my vision suddenly cleared. My goals changed. Children once again appeared as just that—children, the future of our society. Teachers, staff, and community volunteers were recognized as the assets they are—tools to assist in developing the strengths that are present in each student. As I met with my cohort group each week, we would discuss ideas and writings by authors such as Freire or Starratt. Generally, topics addressed writings concerning democracy and authenticity, but more importantly, and just as powerful to my practice, we talked about what was taking place on our campuses. We often had particular children on our minds and we needed advice or guidance on how to best help in some situation or another. Sometimes the needs were academic. Often, as we studied and talked and reflected, we wondered how to assist families in becoming more informed of their role in the educational process. My paradigm was beginning to change from focusing on numbers to caring for students. I began to use a new lens to view the educational responsibility of a campus leader.

TIPPING POINTS OF THE HEART

As we studied how to build authentic learning communities as described by Dufour and Fullan, I began to understand that schools are about much more than accountability standards and state rankings. The purpose of a school system is about educating children, all children, not only with academics but also with values, care, and realization of self-worth. Within this newfound relationship to knowledge, Jenlink (2001) suggests a "new epistemology" of practice evolves, leading to the practice of offering "new opportunities for learners to learn" (p. 12). Gladwell (2000) tells us little changes make big differences. There is always the possibility small events will bring about sudden and infinite change. The term for this phenomenon is the "tipping point." In education, we must be aware of this change moment taking place in order to unlock the potential in students as they enter a campus where they feel safe, cared for, and able to risk becoming part of the learning community.

One morning a fourth-grade student was brought to my office for disciplinary reasons. She was not completing her work and continued to talk and disrupt class after repeated teacher attempts to refocus her behavior. She had been placed in a bilingual class for students who were mostly new to the campus. After discussing the rules and consequences of her behavior, I found that she had been on campus since kindergarten and had not been exited from this predominantly Spanish-instructed classroom, even though her English skills were developed. Evidently, the previous administrators only saw the behaviors and not the possibilities that could allow this child to interact appropriately in a classroom that was more academically focused instead of specifically vocabulary based.

As I talked to this young lady, a need was revealed to provide her with a more challenging instructional placement instead of disciplinary action to remedy her behavior. She had evidently fallen through the cracks academically because of her behavior, which was fueled by boredom. Assuring her of her potential and ability to be successful in the regular classroom not only provided her with an expectation and goals but also let her know someone believed in her abilities to succeed. Taking time to place her in classrooms with caring teachers and a strong mentor provided her the knowledge and motivation, not just to learn English but also to realize she could fit into the mainstream of education. Her behavior and academics improved, and I saw the results of taking time to get to know students and their situations before rushing to dispense discipline for behaviors not conducive to learning. This was a tipping point not only for the student but also for me as an administrator.

Tipping points become transformation points for educational leaders when they are acknowledged and used as directives for future practice. Maxwell (2004) challenges us, "Focus on each child as an individual . . . one person at a time. Make these children understand they are special and capable of learning and succeeding" (p. 45). The doctoral program has instilled in me the need to look for those moments when I need to focus on the individual, finding the moment that makes possible changes that last a lifetime.

INVITING THE FAMILY

Payne (1998) pointed out the need for support systems for parents and students. Often the school is the safest and most welcoming place the family knows to turn to in times of need. Using my new lens of criticality, I recognized areas where programs already in place could be enhanced to better support students on our campus and their families, developing a community of learners. Now, our campus employs a social worker available to assist in answering questions about housing or medical needs. Previously, her main focus was truancy. There was little or no follow-up on why the student was not in class or how we could help ensure attendance. A technology lab had been set up to provide tutoring for parents working on English language skills. While this was previously offered, now special attention is paid to the time we are available to parents, making sure we accommodate work schedules and offering babysitting services if necessary.

Deal and Kennedy (1982) emphasized how the important trait of connecting to each other, which is found in successful organizations, adds meaning and purpose to each other's lives. This was made especially clear to me one morning when a parent arrived in the school office. Speaking no English, she told our social worker that she needed help paying the electric bill. She kept saying she feared not having access to a breathing machine in case of an asthma attack. We assumed she was concerned for the health of one of her four children who were new to our campus from Mexico. She had no money and no relatives living nearby, and the only hope of help was friends in El Paso.

Phone calls to the local electric company and Love, Inc., a Christian assistance organization, soon had her assured of at least four weeks of electricity. Our social worker explained to her where to sign up for additional assistance and how to begin to look for employment in our town. After all of this activity to help one of our students, we suddenly realized through our conversation with the parent that she was the one in need of the breathing machine, not one of the children. It made no difference; our efforts would have been the same. We were pleased to have been viewed as a source of help, not only for students but also for the extended family. After all, we are a learning community, not exclusively a student-based system. Previously, I would have asked the social worker to give the parent the name of some charitable organizations, but armed with my newfound sense of social justice, I felt a responsibility to become involved with taking care of this situation with dignity and respect for the family.

Donaldson (2001) challenges educators regarding "living and working in collaboration" (p. 91). This requires a shared effort and vision, giving up of power, and demonstrating a willingness to invest one's own time and effort into reaching out to students on the campus and in the community to reach certain goals. In order for effective and lasting change to occur, campus leaders must embrace this philosophy. The return on this investment is well worth the effort.

My involvement exhibited the extent to which I valued those involved with the children's education from the home standpoint. Would the outcome have been the same without me? Of course. The social worker is trained in these situations. Would the relationship of care between the family and me have been established? No, and that makes all the difference. After this meeting, the parent was often seen on campus with her children. She was able to find work and did not have to ask for any more help. What a powerful moment in my practice that I almost missed!

FINDING THE KEY

Since beginning the doctoral program, my definition of a successful campus has changed. It has expanded. Academics continue to have center stage, but the manner in which they are approached has changed. Realizing the importance of teaching to a student's strengths instead of focusing on weaknesses is one area of change in my mindset. Welcoming the things students and parents can add to a campus is another way to develop a campus climate conducive to learning. Now, on days of celebration, such as Christmas, Cinco de Mayo, or Kwanzaa, families in classrooms add to the learning as they share their experience, as well as wonderful ethnic foods that represent their culture.

As a campus leader, I found that participating in community events such as the Martin Luther King Memorial March downtown and the

Cinco de Mayo Festival allowed me to become better acquainted with parents and develop relationships. There were so many opportunities to build relationships with families and community when I joined together with them for a common cause, whether it was celebrating a holiday or raising funds for new playground equipment. Last year I volunteered to work at the Cinco de Mayo Festival sponsored by the Hispanic Chamber of Commerce in our town. I was definitely a minority that morning as I assisted in setting up booths and food kiosks.

However, that morning as I assisted with the Bouncing Booth, a large inflated plastic room with netting around the sides, my ethnicity was of no consequence to the good times everyone was sharing. Things were going great and my customers were enjoying jumping and laughing within the confines of netting and plastic inflatable tubing. Suddenly, the compressor hose slipped out of the housing and the structure began to collapse as the air failed to make connection with the pipes. Fearfully, I looked around for help evacuating my charges. Within seconds, community members and parents surrounded me. Our main focus was helping take care of the children and assisting in holding the connectors of the compressor and booth together until all participants were safely out of harm's way. We then joined in for a laugh at the sudden excitement while repairs were taking place. Vendors shared cool drinks with us and I was awarded a T-shirt for going above and beyond my usual responsibility. I experienced acceptance and a feeling of camaraderie for a day of shared experiences and joy that I would have missed if I had not been willing to join in the "community" of my students and their families.

As I reflect back on this experience, there is no recollection of cultural or ethnic background of those jumping in the booth at the time of the catastrophe, nor of those who helped prevent disaster. In a moment of need, our cultures and lifestyles easily merged as we cared for each other without hesitation.

The appreciation shown by the festival coordinators and my students' parents provided insight and enjoyment as I shared a day with people who care for their children as I am learning to care for them on a daily basis. Education is about working together toward shared goals for student success with commitment and purpose. This should become the norm, not the extraordinary.

NEW OPPORTUNITIES

Freire (2001) discusses the idea of "unfinishedness" making us "responsible beings" (p. 56). My realization of how important this "becoming" is occurred last summer as I worked in a different type of summer program. Previously, I had served as principal for an academic summer school, but this past summer, it was my duty to supervise a summer school for mentally and physically challenged children. I thought I had a good understanding of my duties and planned to attend the summer sessions to allow teachers and staff opportunities to get to know and respect me as a supervisor. I certainly did not entertain "becoming" anything more than I was, a supervisor for special programs for the school district. I knew my job expectations and intended to fulfill those diligently with the summer program as an extra activity in my day. My experiences were very different from those I was expecting.

It had been my intention to show up and check attendance, make sure teachers had their supplies, and return to my office. Daily interaction with students and staff united by a spirit of care and acceptance of all instilled in me a desire to become more aware and involved with this program. As it turned out, I was the one who grew to trust and respect the summer staff. I made it a point to be on-site as the buses delivered students from Lufkin State School, group homes, and public schools served by Lufkin ISD special services. These children ranged in age from 3 years to 17 years. Some were in need of physical therapy, one was blind, five were autistic, two were in wheelchairs, and one would not survive to return next summer. All of these children were attending the program because they were in need of experiences in care, authentic learning, and the joy of feeling valued and successful in their educational processes.

Those who could walk helped push those in wheelchairs. When one of the autistic children would fixate and rock, the other children and staff would continue their activities until their friend was ready to rejoin the group. We all came together as a summer family on our outings to the zoo, airport, and library. We entered many gates bravely during this summer experience and excitedly anticipated what awaited us on the other side. What a sight we must have been! A group of young, old, black, brown, and white individuals walking, some pushing strollers and wheelchairs, some pulling wagons with children riding inside, and one using a tiny walker modified for a four-year-old exploring the world, learning together, and sharing the joy of each accomplishment. During this time, many gates were unlocked for us physically and intrinsically. We joined in the seeking of opportunities for individuals to grow, not just academically, but in exploration of the world surrounding them. Children played at a local water park and experienced the "whoosh" of an airplane taking flight before their eyes during a visit to the airport. These children had too often been relegated to sitting in a portable building awaiting the bus to take them back to their placement home instead of becoming part of the learning experience. These summer experiences unlocked their gates of learning, allowing a more clear understanding of the world around them.

The patience and untiring resolve of these teachers and the students' dedication to do their best each day to meet the expectations set before them enlightened me about how far I had to go to "become" the administrator I hoped to be. I had much to learn as I entered the gates of summer learning. This led me to a richer and deeper understanding of justice and education for all children. Sometimes it was academic, but often it was of a deeper and more meaningful nature. Those involved with the summer program were certainly willing to enter the gates of education and meet the challenge each day to meet the needs of children, equipped with a desire to instill civic courage and democratic zeal while offering opportunities for all to learn life lessons this summer.

INVITING THE FUTURE

Each day as I placed the key into the locks of my campus gates, I made a decision to invite children into the world of education. Since I began this journey toward a doctoral degree, I have also unlocked personal gates allowing me to enter into the realm of educational realization through discourse and practice. This has led to a deeper understanding of the concepts and ideals that not only shape academic minds but also shape true and responsible hearts. I am not only entrusted with the keys to the gates of my campus but also with the keys that will help lead these children to successful and productive futures. Each of us has a responsibility to allow education to unlock the doors of opportunity, ensuring that the prison doors of mis-education are opened, and that the doors to knowledge are accessible and inviting to all. One day, the students of today will become the key holders for others. The gates must be opened for all of us in order to sustain a society of democracy and justice, as well as a community of lifelong learners. I remind myself of this daily. I unlock gates to the future.

Sherry Durham is a special programs supervisor for Lufkin Independent School District in Lufkin, Texas.

THE METAMORPHOSIS OF CARING

Nelda Wellman

You find your way by opening your eyes. And your heart.

—Bolman & Deal (2001, p. 31)

Butterflies are nature's true magicians. During their lifetime they have the ability to transform three times in a process called metamorphosis. The caterpillar of some kinds of butterflies wraps itself in silk for a protective covering before it changes into a chrysalis. One can hardly see any changes outside the chrysalis, but inside a major change takes place. Some butterflies only need a few days for this to occur, while other species may take as long as a few years! When the development is completed, the pupa's skin dries and breaks, allowing the adult butterfly to emerge. There it stays on a branch until its wings are dry and it is ready to fly.

A requirement for this insect to be able to fly is a change in weight, simply because caterpillars are much too heavy to fly. Another characteristic that dramatically changes is the eyesight. The caterpillar has six simple eyes permitting only limited and poor eyesight, while the butterfly has compound eyes enabling it to have excellent eyesight. So many differences exist between caterpillars and butterflies that it is difficult to believe they are the same insect. It is incredibly complicated to understand how the caterpillar inside its new pupal case changes itself into a butterfly. Yet this metamorphosis stage provides protection from predators and elements beyond the control of the developing butterfly while it undergoes incredible change within the safe haven of the chrysalis. Perhaps you are wondering what all of this has to do with participating in a doctoral program, but it does . . . for I have been and will be continuing to go through the phase of metamorphosis.

THE BEGINNING OF METAMORPHOSIS

Continuing my graduate studies, wrapped in my silk cocoon, comfortable with my educational practices, I was at ease with myself. I felt prepared to apply my previous knowledge and experiences into the coursework. Little did I comprehend that much of my foundational knowledge and practices would be challenged, scrutinized, criticized, analyzed, and publicized, only to be reconstructed into a deeper search for meaning, self-analysis, and a renewed sense of destiny.

Like the caterpillar still in its pupa, the growing pains began that first weekend of class. We were asked to read articles written by such authors as Foster, Anderson, and Giroux and to explore the critical issues in education and how these issues are handled in practice. The writings of Wheatley particularly began to resonate and speak to my heart, and a passion to understand the true definition and nature of caring teachers began to emerge. Questions such as the following needed answers: Why did some teachers appear to be more caring than others? Was this an inborn trait or a trait of spirituality, not in the religious sense but in the true meaning of interconnectedness? Are there degrees or levels of caring?

Wheatley (2002) defined the caring leader when she spoke of the interconnection that all feel about life and noted that in making decisions, leaders need to be aware of the effects on others. She challenged leaders to "act on this truth when we're willing to notice how a decision might affect others, when we try to think systemically, when we're willing to look down the road and notice how, at this moment, we might be affecting future generations" (p. 44). She continued with this idea and argued that when leaders think past the immediate time and themselves, they are acknowledging that "there's more to life than just us" (p. 45). This sounded much like a convicting sermon that spoke volumes and resonated so deeply within that I could no longer be satisfied to remain in my isolated cocoon. Something began happening; the metamorphosis had begun.

In my research readings I found that Doyle and Doyle (2003) acknowledged that all schools are concerned about the academic progress of their students, but "schools that are caring communities go beyond core content to the psychological and social well-being of their students" (p. 260). Most people can identify a teacher in their life who had a positive and profound impact upon their life. This is not because of the content or information the teacher shared, but generally of the memory of "a caring human being who chose to invest in our learning" (Bolman & Deal, 2001, p. 208). This implied that acts of caring for the psychological and social well-being of the student could lead to more effective teaching and even more effective student learning.

I questioned the natural responses of students who felt cared for by a teacher compared to those who did not. Then Freire (1998) opened my eyes to several areas that are important in the critical educational practice. In his opinion, students should "engage in the experience of assuming themselves as social, historical, thinking, communicating, transformative, creative persons" (p. 45). In addition, students should feel they are "dreamers of possible utopias, capable of being angry because of a capacity to love" (p. 45). Eloquently, Freire described the caring teacher with these words:

> It is fundamental for us to know that without certain qualities or virtues such as a generous loving heart, respect for others, tolerance, humility, a joyful disposition, love of life, openness to what is new, a disposition to welcome change, perseverance in the struggle, a refusal of determinism, a spirit of hope, and openness to justice, progressive pedagogical practice is not possible. (p. 108)

These teacher characteristics could surely model for students an ethic of care that would create "dreamers of possible utopias."

PERCEPTION OF CARING DURING METAMORPHOSIS

The caterpillar has six simple eyes permitting only limited and poor eyesight. Not only does it have limited vision but also limited movement and capabilities. Its primary focus is the area in which it was born and it does not concern itself with things going on around it. At this point in the life cycle of this insect, it is preparing and developing to move into the next cycle of its life.

So it was with the initial caring that I had as a teacher in the early years of my teaching. My focus was primarily limited to my own particular classroom and I was rarely concerned with what was going on outside those walls. My vision was limited, with little or no knowledge of issues that exerted influences on the behaviors of children. My primary goal as a teacher was to teach content while seeking to be fair, equitable, and just in the management of my classroom. It was my opinion that what happened outside the classroom was not the teacher's concern, because, after all, I was unable to change the situation. Still, I did not feel comfortable that students, especially elementary students, should suffer consequences due to inappropriate actions of parents and other adults.

This was exemplified in homework issues that happened repeatedly. In my practice before entering the doctoral program, I failed to consider reasons that a child might not be able to complete homework without providing the child other options. Rather, I became frustrated and tended to scold and apply consequences. After reading and discussing social justice that included caring, fairness, equity, and justice, I analyzed my own practices to conclude that many changes were needed. These included finding out more about the children through listening to the things they said about their home life and their family.

Kerrick was an eight-year-old student of mine whose primary caregiver was an alcoholic mother; he never completed his homework. He was the youngest of many brothers, was rearing himself alone, and most evenings had no evening meal. His life outside of school was concerned more with survival than schoolwork. Before I understood his life, I was extremely frustrated with him. As I learned about his very dysfunctional family life, I realized that he needed additional support in order to complete homework. When he learned that I was willing to work with him, he began to come to class earlier and work on homework. Through this arrangement, we both accomplished our goals and Kerrick was encouraged when he found that he could work successfully at school, despite unfortunate outside influences.

THE METAMORPHOSIS OF CARING

As I began to understand the wider possibilities of the caring teacher, I considered my practice in working with elementary children who were often late to school. In the past, a child who was consistently late to my class was given consequences that usually meant working on makeup work during recess. I did not usually question the reason. As I began to develop a clearer and deeper understanding of caring from many of our readings and class discussions, I noted that my attitude toward this problem became one of desire to be equitable and just, and more caring.

Matt, a very active intelligent nine-year-old student, was continually late for school, ranging from 15 minutes to an hour. I spoke with his mother and Matt repeatedly about the problem and some improvement would occur for a short time. Finally out of desperation, I talked with Matt privately about his home life. There was a new baby in the family and Matt was responsible for getting himself up and ready for school. His stepfather was responsible for calling from work to awaken Matt. Many mornings the father would forget to do so and, of course, Matt would oversleep. He was suffering the embarrassment and negative consequences of arriving at school late because of the irresponsible behaviors of adults. My actions needed to show how much I cared for Matt. From that point on, Matt would sign in at the office and slip quietly into the classroom receiving a nod and a smile from me. This assured Matt that he was welcome and that I understood his problem. Additionally, I chose to help Matt make up work that he had missed during another time period, but not at recess. He became happier at school and worked hard to produce good work in return. My metamorphosis was continuing.

Caring exhibited by classroom teachers is essential for developing relationships between the student and the teacher. Caring teachers encourage the student to make a commitment to school and to learning, which can ultimately serve as an encouragement and a motivation to all students, regardless of their diverse backgrounds.

Further, teacher caring has a significant effect on academic performance, attendance, and positive behavior. Trusting relationships with teachers encourage risk taking that is necessary for learning. These relationships help students to connect school with their future. When students feel that the teacher has acknowledged their home and culture, they respond with greater success (Perez, 2000).

FREEDOM TO CARE

Unlike the limited eyesight of the caterpillar, the butterfly has compound eyes enabling it to have excellent eyesight. Additionally, before metamorphosis, this insect is unable to fly. During the pupa stage, wings are developed, allowing the matured butterfly to fly soon after it emerges. Its environment is no longer limited to a small area from which it feeds but, instead, it has the freedom to move freely and to varying heights. With excellent eyesight and this capability to move about, the butterfly has a broadened picture of the surroundings from which it is able to gain sustenance.

Just as the butterfly enlarges its surroundings through growth as the result of metamorphosis, so I expanded my horizons as a result of participating in a doctoral program. This has resulted in an exploration and an analysis of the person that I really am. Kincheloe and Steinberg (1999) noted that people are never free of the social and past influences that make us but, instead, we are a part of that reality and cannot be separated from them. Reflecting on the philosophical nature of life led me to a personal search of my own identity. As a result of my growing critical awareness, I began to understand that caring, in the deepest sense, cannot truly exist without authenticity and courage. By understanding my own weaknesses and critically reflecting on my ways of dealing with situations, I am daily becoming more perceptually aware of the need to forgive the weaknesses of others. This becomes a part of the caring exhibited toward all people, especially children.

Not only did this growing understanding of myself and my students create in me a need to be compassionate but it also fostered a need to become authentic. I found that as I truly included the qualities of authenticity into every existence of my life, it became an observable part of caring, with actions that included equity and justice. Through authenticity and other complementary characteristics, as a caring teacher I became more skilled in developing and fostering deeper and more lasting relationships with not only my students but also with fellow faculty, the parents, and the community. My metamorphosis is continuing.

CARING AS A CIVIC NECESSITY

As my personal and professional metamorphosis continues and my understanding of the care ethic deepens, I realize that civic courage is necessary. This type of caring requires me to consider the larger picture of what children often experience outside the classroom, as well as within the classroom. Harris (2004) explained the importance of courage by saying, "Sometimes advocating for students not only takes courage, but also requires tremendous energy, as we consider the battles needed to be fought to do what we consider is best for them" (p. 81).

To accept this challenge of actively caring takes courage and a willingness to take action. Donaldson (2001) believes this type of person must "literally care enough to take action despite objections and discomfort" (p. 144). Often these caring acts lead to the "butterfly effect." Wheatley (2002) explained that the cause and effect of the flapping of butterfly wings in Japan causes hurricanes to occur. This idea supports the concept of the interconnectedness of systems. In like manner, my personal metamorphosis created in me the aspiration of becoming interconnected with others, providing the leadership for demonstrating what true caring is all about. Just as in the butterfly effect, the small, individual acts of caring may not always seem to produce immediate visible results, but over time and collectively they produce powerful results.

This larger concept of caring has led me to question what I can do to make a difference in the lives of children and not just those whom I teach or directly influence. The following is a sample list that has become my beginning point of challenge:

- Actively participate in parent-teacher organizations
- Develop relationships with parents of students
- Learn about the child I teach outside the classroom
- Become an advocate for age-appropriate media for children
- Learn about the relationship of TV violence and children
- Keep current with legislation involving children
- Contact legislators regarding policies with negative influences

I have heard many people use the phrase, "Oh! Children are resilient. They bounce back!" While I am confident that many children are resilient, still any emotional or physical abuse or neglect, whether intentional or unintentional, leaves scars that remain for life. When enough of those scars accumulate, they can begin to surface in the form of suicide, depression, bulimia, drug abuse, or violent behaviors. If by caring deeply I can help one child who might otherwise have no hope, what a marvelous and miraculous gift . . . for both of us.

CONCLUSION

Each spring I buy begonia baskets to hang on my patio. I don't have a lot of time to care for them and usually by the end of June they are beginning to wilt for lack of care. Last year, at some point in the summer, a wind blew one of the baskets down into a mound of Asian jasmine that is underneath the tree. I walked past that tree several times with the intentions of throwing the basket away but I never did. Recently, I looked out my back window and saw the most beautiful red begonia flowers blooming among the jasmine. All winter, the begonia had lain protected and cared for by the jasmine that surrounded it. Buried and protected in the richness of the deep earth, it had access to more soil than that of the planter and now was blooming more vibrantly than ever before. Soon, butterflies will land on its blooms to nourish their flight. Just as the soil had nourished the begonia, and just as the cocoon had protected the butterfly, authentic caring teachers nourish and protect children to grow the wings of their independence. Being a caring teacher helps me be part of this process by providing the hope and encouragement needed to become a productive and excited lifelong learner. The metamorphosis continues.

Nelda Wellman currently teaches third grade for the Newton ISD in Newton, Texas.

MY STORY, MY SONG: REFLECTIONS INSPIRED BY THE PROCESS

Perry Daniel

A form of education grounded in a notion of educational leadership . . . does not begin with the quest for raising test scores, but with a moral and political vision of what it means to educate students to govern, lead a humane life, and address the social welfare of those less fortunate than themselves. This is a notion of leadership that dreams in order to change the world rather than simply manage it.

—Giroux (1994, p. 45)

The doctoral program experience has truly been interesting for me. As I struggled to complete assignments during the spring 2004 semester, I felt like I was being hazed. After the semester ended, I assessed the entire year and can only compare this process to pledging a Greek letter organization. With that in mind, the professors were the big brothers and big sisters and the cohort members were my line brothers and line sisters. Our big brothers and big sisters, as with their equals in Greek organizations, were the source of some joy and a great deal of pain. Even though our endurance and mental ability were tested by our professors' expectations, they were patient and guided us through this stage of the process.

Our cohort is similar to a line of pledges. We came together from different cultures, with different philosophies, with the desire and determination to complete a common goal. The variety of beliefs, personalities, and experiences of each member added value to our cohort's worth. On several occasions during this process, some members have put their personal agendas aside to support decisions of the cohort. Throughout the year we have supported one another as if we were brothers and sisters, helping each other through tough assignments, exchanging e-mails and calls as some of us experienced family crises, and attending the numerous advice/professional counseling sessions that were held to help all of us become better educational leaders. We are truly a strong line of pledges and I am sure we will complete this journey together.

I learned more about myself during this period of academic growth than I would have in any other setting. Successful leaders have a keen sense of self-knowledge and use this as a foundation to learn about and to lead others. I describe my evolution as a doctoral student and scholar-practitioner leader in four areas: 1) courage, conviction, and commitment, 2) relationships, 3) authenticity, and 4) reflection. I am an unfinished piece of work and know that my evolution is a never-ending progression.

Bennett (2000) in *Forced into Glory: Abraham Lincoln's White Dream* described how "Honest Abe" has been glorified for signing the Emancipation Proclamation and freeing the slaves, when in reality not a single slave was freed by this legislation. Referring to the title *Forced into Glory*, but not to Abraham Lincoln, it is a true depiction of my development and status in the cohort. I must admit that I entered the program with selfish intentions. I was only thinking about what I could do with "Dr." before my name. The selfishness of my desires left my heart when I started this program and the term *scholar-practitioner leader* was discussed in both the theoretical and practical contexts. The fact that I was the only Black student in my cohort also changed my perspective and caused me to realize that in order to be a true scholar-practitioner I would have to live and practice unselfishly. Because of the demographics of the cohort, I was forced into the position of representative of my race and accepted the challenge of destroying racial stereotypes and improving the educational experience of all students at all levels, but specifically Black (African American) students. Freire (1993) suggested that education is the key to freedom. I want to accomplish what Lincoln had the power to do but did not do: I want to free my people.

As I mentioned earlier, my thought process changed when I realized that I was the lone Black in the cohort. One of my cohort members asked me, "Were you nervous or intimidated when you walked in and saw that you were the only Black student in the cohort?" I simply responded no and asked, "Why should I have been intimidated?" I didn't get much of a reply. I wanted to ask if she would have been afraid or nervous if the numbers were reversed. I actually answered this question during a class discussion on another date. I had described to the class how Blacks have to assimilate into their culture, so being the minority in a group was nothing new to me. I also expressed to my cohort that I am a strong Black man and proud of who I am, and explained to them the biases and challenges that I face on a regular basis are difficult. These challenges assist in building my character, integrity, and courage as I attempt to attack the ills of society and educational systems.

COURAGE, CONVICTION, AND COMMITMENT

I am becoming more aware of issues of education and race. Recently I watched the *Tavis Smiley Show* on PBS and his guest for the evening was Bill Cosby. Smiley questioned Cosby concerning controversial comments he made about Blacks, education, and economic status. The next morning on the *Tom Joyner Morning Show*, a nationally broadcast radio show, Smiley reflected on his conversation with Cosby and described him with three words: courage, conviction, and commitment. Smiley concluded that Cosby is courageous for speaking out, is passionate about education, and has proven his commitment to the education of Blacks by providing millions of dollars to support historically Black colleges and universities. The actions of my practice must signify my conviction, courage, and commitment to the field of education and the students, teachers, and parents that I have the opportunity to impact.

Courage

One of our professors reminded us often during our first summer that the scholar-practitioner leader possesses courage. I often focused on this area in my daily practice because it was one of my weaknesses before I started the program. I work to improve this part of my practice by accepting challenging tasks, such as talking to irate parents, dealing with troublesome teachers, and discussing controversial but important issues. I can see myself growing in this area.

Not only am I the minority in class but I also am the minority at my job. I have learned that in both environments I must have the courage to speak up for what is right. In the first class of the fall semester, one of my cohort members made a statement in reference to African Americans, babies, and politics during a brief presentation. Some of the other cohort members perceived the comment to be offensive to me. I was not offended by the comment but it was not tactful (nor was it what we discussed in our group before the presentation). After class I explained to my cohort member that he did not offend me, but if he did, I would make him aware of it.

The second incident occurred on my job. I was telling a teacher about my planned research on the achievement gap. She implied that Black students perform lower because of the traditional foods (chitterlings, black-eyed peas, etc.) they eat on New Year's Day. I responded, "No, I don't think that's it. I think it has more to do with what is going on at school and in the classroom." The next day I called the teacher to my office and explained to her that those types of statements and thoughts are the main contributors to the achievement gap. I also cautioned her that statements of that nature could hurt feelings and have professional ramifications.

These two events display my courage to speak against acts that are unkind and borderline racist. These types of comments have no place in the field of education. Giroux (1994) suggests that educational leaders should dream of changing the world, not just managing it. In order to live this dream and accomplish the task of uplifting African American students and educators, I can no longer be passive when addressing statements and issues of injustice and inequity, nor can I avoid addressing undemocratic practices. As a scholar-practitioner I have to use my self-knowledge and place myself in positions to change the world.

Conviction and Commitment

Freire (1998) described his lifelong fight for equity and justice for oppressed groups as a conviction. One of my best friends and mentor told me that in obtaining a doctoral degree, it was my duty to help African American children. My conviction and commitment are aimed at improving the plight of the African American educator and student in the educational systems of America. I realize the seriousness and complexity of this task. I am also realistic in thinking that this is a lifelong duty and it will not be completed in 5 to 10 years.

In order to accomplish my goal, I must perfect the practice of altruistic living. In every facet of my life I need to give until it hurts and then give just a little more. For the students, I have to be a role model and give them examples of how to deal with growing up in America. To the educators, I have to be a quality leader who displays good communication skills and a genuine concern for their well-being. And for myself, I have to stay focused on my mission and accept that the true rewards will come from the successes of students and educators that I influence.

RELATIONSHIPS

Being in a doctoral program has helped me realize the importance of building strong positive working relationships. Many of the readings and discussions were instrumental in helping me change the manner in which I interact with people, both at work and elsewhere. Now I realize the importance of communication and expressions of appreciation as keys to building strong relationships in our field.

I borrowed some ideas from some of my cohort members and implemented them at my school. For example, at my school we were experiencing a case of Unappreciated Teacher Syndrome. I had to do something to let the teachers know that the administration cared about them and that we knew they were working hard. I took advice from a classmate who had talked about small incentives he had given his teachers. I provided a cooler of Red Bull and Gatorade for the faculty. I attached a note to the cooler that stated, "Thanks for your hard work and effort. Use these to restore your energy." Although many of the faculty didn't take me up on the offer, several of them came by and expressed their thanks for this thoughtful act. I just wanted to show them that they were appreciated.

AUTHENTICITY

Authenticity starts with the knowledge of self. When Dr. Robert J. Starratt, author and professor at Boston College, spoke to our classes, he discussed the ethics of authenticity of the educational leader. He stated, "The authentic educational leader unceasingly cultivates an environment which promotes the work of authentic teaching and learning." It is in my practice that I choose to do things differently than others. I have to make decisions that allow me to sleep at night. From some of my cohort members I have learned that it is better to sleep on a decision and make the right decision than to make decisions hastily.

Before starting the doctoral program, I would allow myself to get caught up in other people's emotions and make quick decisions. I have learned patience through my experiences in this program. Although I understand the importance of making decisions in a timely manner, any decision that doesn't involve the safety of my students and faculty can be determined after a discussion or a good night's rest.

Duffy (2003) noted the impact of authentic leadership on trust. An authentic leader looks at himself or herself introspectively, and examines his or her own ability to provide honest and constant feedback to others, to foster diversity, to nurture teamwork and collaboration, and to acknowledge and encourage informal networks among others. But the test of authenticity comes down to a simple question: Are these leaders walking their talk? I must make sure that I lead by example. I am who I am and my practice must be my authentic practice.

Sometimes my thoughts in some areas are viewed as radical in the field of education. My opinions on student dress code policies or responses to certain behaviors of students and teachers tend to differ from some of my peers. In our cohort, several of us have similar educational philosophies but we also display some distinct differences. One difference is our choice of music, which may be due to our various cultures or differences in age. My interest in today's music found its way into my

MY STORY, MY SONG

doctoral program in a reflection that I wrote. Our professor had just returned from Ireland and was discussing some of the historical sights he saw on his trip. He emphasized seeing a castle that was owned by a member of the band U2. Here is a portion of my journal entry from one of our classes in the fall.

> I listened to the discussion about U2 and their history. I wonder if I can break the mold?
> Will I ever share information and will students make reference to hip-hop artists, the music, or the culture? Being that I am a product of this culture, I wish I could assess the impact of this culture on education.

While there are some negative impacts of the hip-hop culture on the youth of today, there are also some positive elements. Hip-hop is a part of me and influences the lives of so many of our kids and some of our teachers. I want to be authentic in implementing strategies to make the impact a positive one.

Recently, while working summer school, I had an opportunity to incorporate some lyrics from the hip-hop duo Outkast to make a point to some students. The students were four African American young men. One of them complained, "The security coordinator and the deputy are always tripping. They are always trying to get us in trouble." I was aware that there was some validity to the young man's statement. Both of the security men were African American and their daily focus was generally more on degrading the kids rather than uplifting them. The kids were puzzled by the words and actions of these gentlemen because they were also African American. In quoting Outkast, I stated "Is every brother with dreads for the cause? Naw. Is every brother with golds for the fall? So don't get caught up in appearance." I attempted to explain to the young men that just because someone is African American does not mean that he has their best interests at heart. I expressed to them that they should learn from this experience and understand that the true character of a person is not determined by appearance or ethnicity. That brief conversation solidified my thoughts that we and our students can both learn from hip-hop.

Through my continuous education I began to notice that authenticity is evident in my personal life as well. Although I have always possessed the trait of authenticity, I didn't always describe it as such. As a teenager

I would have described it as having my own style. As a young adult I would have just identified it as being cool. And as a doctoral student I describe it as authenticity. My authenticity was presented in the simplest form recently. I was having a conversation with a friend of mine who made a thought-provoking comment about my tennis shoes. His comment implied that my Nikes were outdated. I responded by noting that I own some new styles of shoes also. I also told him, "I am going to do me; you do you." Dr. Starratt and the music of hip-hop artist Jay-Z inspired my response.

REFLECTION

Another component of doctoral work is continuous reflection. Teachers should reflect on their lives to improve their practice and interaction with students and other teachers. The same is true of administrators and other educational leaders. I have started to seriously reflect on the events in my life by writing a journal. Reflecting is the perfect means for documenting my wonderful experiences as an assistant principal. Not only does reflecting provide the opportunity to assess my actions and thoughts, but it can also provide a laugh when I am experiencing tough times. The following is from my November 14, 2003, journal entry. The entry is entitled "Sleeping Maturation." It reads,

> I wrote the following lines as a participant in Jeff's presentation on the Art Inquiry Methods:
>> I am so tired but I continue to grow.
>> All these new methods, its enriching I know.
>> The methods and more research will grow into a dissertation.
>> No sleep, writing and learning, the theory of sleeping maturation.

This particular journal entry represented my feelings after completing a large assignment, getting two hours of sleep, working all day, and then having to sit in class for three hours. Journal reflection was introduced originally as an assignment but has become an essential part of my practice and personal life.

CONCLUSION

My experiences as a doctoral student have truly helped me evolve as a scholar-practitioner leader. From these experiences I am confident that I chose the right career and that the education profession is the arena in which I must return so many of the blessings that have been given to me. I would like to conclude with two thoughts. The first one is a quote that motivates me to give the students my best and to be an example for other educators. The quote reads, "One hundred years from now . . . it will not matter what my bank account was, the sort of house I lived in, or the kind of car I drove, but the world may be different because I was important in the life of a child," by an unknown author.

The second thought is of the word *namaste*, which means, "the God in me sees and honors the God in you" (Beals, 1995, p. 222). The people, the students, and the teachers are often forgotten in this era of high-stakes testing and accountability. I value my interaction with these two groups. When it is all said and done, I will be held accountable by a being much higher than school administrators and state boards of education, and that higher being is much more important to me.

RECOMMENDATIONS

There are three factors that helped me to experience some success and maintain my sanity while in this first year of my doctoral program. The first factor is God, for answering my prayers and giving me this opportunity. The second is my cohort, for being there and understanding. The third factor is my family and friends, who were very supportive and love me enough to tell me when I am wrong and encouraged me to stay focused. A strong support system is recommended for anyone thinking of entering a doctoral program.

Perry Daniel is principal at a middle school for Caddo Parish School Board in Shreveport, Louisiana.

SPIRITUALITY: ANCHOR OF LEADERSHIP

Wendell Wellman

> We can never assume that anyone else sees the world as we do.
>
> —Wheatley & Kellner-Rogers (1999, p. 49)

As the torrid, late summer heat shimmered through the open windows of the little rural, redbrick schoolhouse, my third-grade teacher's voice wafted through the end-of-school-day drowsiness. She was saying, "Now, remember to ask your parents where they were born and what grade they completed, so we can fill out the federal survey tomorrow morning." I wondered why we had to do the same survey every year. Why couldn't they look in the folder from last year?

Next morning, Mrs. Kerry began roll call and asked each student the yearly questions, "Where were your parents born? What grade did they complete?" When it finally came my turn, I proudly answered that both had completed seventh grade and my dad was born in Texas and my mother was born in Pwan-ah-pee Parish, Louisiana. Mrs. Kerry laughed aloud as my face reddened. The entire class turned to stare at me and snicker. Mrs. Kerry loudly replied, "There is no such place as Pwan-ah-pee Parish! Tonight ask your mother where she was born, and have it right tomorrow."

That night I tried to ask casually, "Mother, where were you born?" She replied in her Cajun drawl, "Sha child, I was born in Pwan-ah-pee

Parish, why you ax?" "Oh, no reason," I replied while contemplating what embarrassment I would face tomorrow at school and wondering why my family had to be so different.

Once again, Mrs. Kerry began the morning roll call with the same drill. Some of the kids had forgotten to ask, and they received a royal tongue-lashing. I thought about lying, but knew that would not help matters any—and then suddenly it was my turn. "Wendell, where was your mother born?" Mrs. Kerry sternly asked. "Pwan-ah-pee Parish, ma'am," I hesitantly replied. Mrs. Kerry's face reddened, "Did you ask your mother?" she shouted. "Yes, ma'am," I whispered. "Did she say Pwan-ah-pee Parish? That is the dumbest thing I have ever heard! There is no parish in the state of Louisiana named Pwan-ah-pee!" she said sneeringly, drawing out the "ah" and emphasizing the "pee" while bulging her eyes. There I sat with my face molten red. I tried to swallow, but my throat was dry. The hair on the back of my neck was singing, and my ears were ringing. The teacher had just called my mother "dumb" and that meant I was dumb.

That evening, I found my dad alone in the barn and told him what had happened at school. I could not tell my mother because I did not want her to know that my teacher thought she was dumb. When I told my dad, I could see that it made him a little angry but he rarely showed any emotions. I knew a lecture was coming when he quietly turned from his work and looked at me. He paused and said, "Son, you are going to be picked on for the rest of your life. Now, you can react two ways, and you have to choose one: You can get a limp wrist and whine because someone mistreats you, or you can get a strong back and hold your head up and show them that you are going to be a better man!" He reached down and hit me on the shoulder in a manly way, and I felt really big. Then he added, "Your mother is not dumb. Some people just don't take the time to understand other people." Little did I realize that I had just witnessed the highest act of spirituality available to humanity—the act of understanding another's hurts, needs, and fears.

SOCIAL JUSTICE, CARING, AND SPIRITUALITY

Until joining the doctoral cohort, I did not comprehend that my father's single act had shaped my concept of social justice, caring, and spirituality.

One year ago, my concept of spirituality was based on some mystical notion of separation of church and state. This suggested that pairing spirituality, social justice, and educational leadership was incongruous and even dissonant (Solomon & Hunter, 2002). Yet, as an educational leader, I felt that something was missing in my practice as a leader. This led me to ask larger questions of my meaning and purpose, including how to find fulfillment. Ultimately, I found that I must look to my philosophy and understanding of what guides my day-to-day life, my spirituality.

Before entering a doctoral program I defined spirituality in the narrow sense of religion and "doing good to thy neighbor." To my surprise, the assigned readings began to explore wonderful new ideas that opened vast horizons for exploration. When I read that all leaders experience the "dark night" of the soul (Wheatley, 2002), I immediately related. That was me—on the edge of burnout and frustration. I was attempting to be a caring leader and I shared my religious faith when asked. Therefore, I thought I was spiritual. But I knew something was missing. During my 30 years in education, I truly attempted to reach out and help in a caring way to every student.

My graduate studies brought me face-to-face with my own social *in*justice and bias. Until recently, my concept of social justice was simply dependent upon the individual's attitude and response. It did not include or consider the external factors that might determine one's attitude toward life. I began to consider that often there were external factors that oppressed and prevented people from realizing the potential within them. Surely one's culture does influence how one views the world (Freire, 1993). Yet the more I question, the more I realize one question generates two more questions. It is so challenging, maddening, thought provoking, stimulating, exhausting, elating, invigorating, and exhilarating to contemplate this broadened understanding of social justice, since it has become fluid and influenced by others.

From a postformal perspective, the greatest task is the task of knowing oneself (Kincheloe & Steinberg, 1999). However, knowing self is neither an easy nor a pleasant task. Often past hurts, pains, and disappointments are buried under scars that have become calloused and yet remain sensitive—and therefore difficult to resolve. Once I opened the hidden door, to explore the secret room of my past actions and present motivations, then awareness of other's needs challenged my preconceived ideas of justice, equity, fairness, authenticity, and caring. As I reflect back, this challenge brought awareness that I may have unintentionally lacked sensitivity toward students, colleagues, and friends, even when I was attempting to do well.

Freire (1993), hooks (2000), and Payne (1998) all argue that one cannot help the poor by just giving. I recall buying three dresses and a pair of shoes for an economically disadvantaged student who was going to represent my instructional subject at a state competition. But when the day arrived to leave for the competition, she did not come. For 20 years, this lack of appreciation on the part of a very polite student puzzled me. Now, through introspection and reflection, I realize that I was the one who had been ungrateful. I had added insult to injury by only giving that which did not matter. While providing a new dress and shoes was important on the surface, this was an easy way to feel that I had supported her. But it was only "surface" help. What had I done to support her efforts in a deeper sense? Could I have found a better way to help her with her clothing needs? All the child had left was her pride. I was attempting to be caring, fair, and equitable, but perhaps I was giving the wrong message to a student who already lacked confidence.

SPIRITUALITY

A question that I must face now and in the future becomes, how can I establish an environment in my school that facilitates every person being given an equitable, fair, respectful, and just opportunity to achieve, with pride, his or her greatest potential? To answer this question implies that educational leaders must become transformative spiritual leaders. In an interview with Dr. Margaret Wheatley (March 20, 2004), she defined spirituality as realizing there is something more than me. I am bigger because I have a human spirit that is far more than the sum of my intellect or physical self. We participate in a world of intrigue and mystery—the feeling of connectedness in the presences of Love (capital L) that takes us outside ourselves. This web of life through connectedness is spirituality.

In an interview with Dr. Robert J. Starratt (November 14, 2003), he defined spirituality as a deep sense of being grounded in a higher power.

It is being present to the most profound realities in one's life, giving depth to relationships. Solomon and Hunter (2002) defined spirituality as "one's meaning system" (p. 38). This includes one's relationship to oneself, to others, and to God. The essence of spirit, according to Oladele (1999) "is at the heart of a meaningful education. Spirit is the spark of life that resides within every human being; it is the connection to the fabric of all life and to the source of all creation" (p. 62). Spirituality is the web of interconnectedness present when one's spirit, in the profound realities of life, connects in a meaningful and empowering relationship to the spirit of another to produce a spark of life. Spirit is the realization of destiny, through caring and love, that recognizes a power greater than one's own. The spark of life is comprehending an empowering challenge to achieve one's potential. Through these writers and others, I broadened my understanding of spirituality and began to consider ways to incorporate spirituality into my practice.

Yet, realistically, in the past, my practice had been characterized by emphasis on management. As Witcher (2003) explained, "Today's educational leader is so busy with responsibilities of administration that little time and effort is given to the task of guiding students to become ethical and moral members of society" (p. 27). Although, Kessler (1999) poignantly argued that despite more than a decade of headlines about a "generation at risk" (p. 50), the void of spiritual guidance and opportunity in the lives of teenagers is still a rarely noticed factor, often contributing to self-destructive and violent behavior. In fact, Lawrence, Jones, and Smith (1999) found that "young people identified their greatest needs as the need to be loved, the need for someone to listen, and the need for acceptance" (p. 23). Drugs, sex, gang violence, and "even suicide may be both a search for connection and meaning and an escape from the pain of not having a genuine source of spiritual fulfillment" (p. 29). Once again, the readings, discussions, and opportunities for personal reflection in the doctoral program developed a keen awareness of the need for real spirituality within my own practice.

Since grasping the concept of spirituality within education, I see the transformation occurring in my practice almost daily. I now approach every problem, whether with students or faculty members, from the perspective that I do not have the answer—they hold the key to their potential spirituality. Therefore, the potential empowers them to face the challenge. Furthermore, when I walk away, I ask myself two questions: 1) Did I really listen and connect to that person? and 2) Did that person feel better about who he or she was when he or she left my presence?

WORKPLACE APPLICATION

I work in one of the most challenging educational settings—I am principal of a school within an adult incarceration setting. Our goals are to prepare men to earn GEDs and to reenter into the free world. Recently, a young offender was sent to my office for failing to complete assignments. With a new understanding of spirituality, I asked why the assignments were not completed. The student stated the usual excuses and then added, "I'm just not smart enough." I looked up the student's IQ, and found that it was 84, with educational achievement scores at the third-grade level. My heart sank as I contemplated how I could help this student feel better about himself and still expect the assignments to be completed. That is when I remembered that I do not hold the key to others' spirituality, yet I can support their effort to find the key to their potential.

Gardner's (1999) multiple intelligences theory, Wheatley's (2002) chaos theory, and Harris' (2004) comments on power swirled through my head. In my mind I could see Harris' quote, "In other words, power is most effective when it is not power *over* but power *to* and power *with*" (p. 8). She further argued that power should be shared with faculty as well as students. In that moment, the question changed from, why didn't you complete your assignments? to, how can he be empowered to see his own potential? I felt my spirit reach out to this student—once I too had been told, "You can't really make it in college." The power to persevere—perhaps that was the key he needed.

Then spirituality began to flow, not my intellect, but the spirit to reach out and interconnect to produce that spark. I asked the student, "What is most important, 'I Will' or IQ? The 'I Will' in you will overcome. Moreover, IQ is the least important thing that exists—after all, who sets the norms? If 50 IQ were the norm, you would be three standard deviations above normal." The spirit of that young man gave a spark that lit up the room. He began to cry, actually to sob. He said, "You mean I'm not stupid?" I replied, "Absolutely not, and whoever told you that lie was dead wrong!" He jumped up, wiped his eyes, and said, "I'm going to write my daddy tonight and tell him this!" as he whirled out of my office and headed for the classroom. I sat there dumbfounded.

The next day the teacher stopped by and said, "I don't know what you did to that student, but you put a fire under him!" I replied, "No, I don't think I did; I think he did it to himself." Within six months, he brought his educational achievement scores up from third-grade level to tenth-grade level and earned a GED. At our semi-annual GED graduation I watched, with a mixture of pride and profound humility, as he wiped the corners of his eyes when he received his certificate. During the graduation ceremony I watched the visitors' section and observed an older couple crying during the entire ceremony. Yes, that was their son!

SPIRITUAL LEADERSHIP

Bolman and Deal (2001) emphasized, "Leading is giving. Leadership is an ethic, a gift of oneself to a common cause, a higher calling. . . . The essence of leadership is not giving things or even providing visions, instead it is offering oneself and one's spirit" (p. 106). Dantley (2003) espoused that principled leadership begins with a careful and critical reflection of one's position on issues of justice, democracy, and fairness. Spiritual leadership is initiated when an individual questions his or her own actions and motives within the framework of justice, democracy, fairness, caring, and commitment. Spirituality is not weakness, but rather, it is strength through humility and guides one when doing the unpleasant tasks inevitability required at times. Spirituality is a paradigmatic paradox to humanistic thinking because that which is freely shared is generously reaped (Suhor, 1999). This is vividly demonstrated when "trust is the foundation for empowerment, for when principals trust others they are liberated to share their power by giving power away" (Harris, 2004, p. 7). When the spirit of interconnectedness joins with another's spirit, empowerment, caring, and trust are transferred.

The other day, a teacher came in for second shift a little late. She was visibly distraught. She entered my office and began telling about a friend just diagnosed with cancer. I was busy and trying to meet a deadline and moreover I had already given freely of myself to both faculty and students during the morning shift. I was feeling a little harried and needed to get a task completed. Then I remembered—what could I give to this staff member? My undivided attention was the only gift I could give at that moment. I laid everything down, pulled off my glasses, and sat intently listening. Sometimes I would nod my head or make a "hm-m-m" sound. After about five minutes of talking she was visibly more relaxed and made a startling statement: "Thanks so much for talking with me; you are always such a help." It was then I realized I had not uttered one word. There was really nothing I could have said that would have been any help. In five minutes, I had given the gift of spirit—my spirit reaching out to connect and communicate simply by listening and nodding.

Harris (2004) explained that principals who "lighten the burden" (p. 15) show their care and concern for teachers and students alike through empowerment. This action of caring transcends the workplace. This sense of spirit becomes bigger than our job. Wheatley (2002) elaborated, "But in a more subtle form, I hear spiritual thinking whenever anyone talks about their work as a vocation or calling" (p. 42). Howe (1995) expressed it this way: "We need to feel that there is something bigger than ourselves that gives meaning and significance to our lives" (p. 79).

Sokolow (2002) emphasized, "Enlightened leadership is grounded in spiritual principles. . . . Enlightened leaders not only know the right things to do and how to do things right, but they do them for the right reasons" (p. 33). He cautioned, "Enlightened leaders are not infallible. They make errors as we all do, but they are growing and continually learning from their experiences" (p. 34). This continued growth—begun in a doctoral leadership program—has provided me with the tools to define the actions I wish to develop. Margaret Wheatley (2002) defined this type of leadership clearly: "As leaders, we act on this truth when we're willing to notice how a decision might affect others, when we try to think systemically, when we're willing to look down the road and notice how, at this moment, we might be affecting future generations" (p. 46). She further argued that any act that takes us past the immediate problem or moment and past our self-protective behaviors acknowledges that there is more to life than just us.

CHAPTER 16

CONCLUSION

As I contemplate my future practice, I am keenly aware that the task of holding a sense of purpose and providing meaning is almost overwhelming. I have found that spiritual scholar-practitioner is an *everyday* and *everywhere* activity, seven days a week, for a lifetime, and in every environment. Spirituality is a bedrock foundation that stands as the steadfast anchor in the chaotic sea of life. The spiritual scholar-practitioner realizes that spirituality is the anchor of the soul (Wheatley, 2002). At some point, chaos and tragedy will invade the life of every educational leader. Wheatley refers to these occurrences as the "dark night" of the soul.

The spiritual scholar-practitioner recognizes there will be times when dogged determination and perseverance must overcome despair—there will be burnout, broken dreams, loss of hope, and questioning of purpose. There will be goals accomplished that once seemed significant, yet will turn to sand and slip from the hand to be scattered by the winds of opposition. The steadfast anchor of spirituality will give assurance that the storms will pass and hope will be born anew. This confident and sure hope gives one the courage to face the challenge of the future.

The spiritual scholar-practitioner must not fear to show spirituality in his humanity. We must be as the proverbial Jacob (Genesis 32:25) of old—as one who has wrestled with a personal angel and won, yet remains crippled by human frailties. By acknowledging human failures, the spiritual leader communicates high expectations of continued improvement. The secure leader admits fallibility and walks with the limp of humanity undergirded by spirituality.

I predict that my future practice will look like a seagull walking with a broken leg. There will be occasions when I will have to limp upon the hot sand of apologies for mistakes made. But that same limp will permit me to soar with authenticity because trust will be renewed; care and commitment will interconnect with spirit, making spiritual leadership a reality.

As a third grader, a teacher embarrassed me by failing to understand or recognize my suffering and discomfort. On that same day, I saw true spirituality modeled by my father when he comforted me. Yet it took many years for me to connect my father's understanding and supportive act to my own spiritual potential to connect in that same way with others.

Two years ago, my mother passed on. While preparing her obituary, we found her birth certificate—she was born in Pointe Coupee Parish, Louisiana. I turned to my son, who had just graduated from LSU with a minor in Cajun-French, and said, "How do you say Pointe Coupee Parish in Cajun-French?" He replied, "Pwan-ah-pee Parish!"

Wendell Wellman currently serves as a principal in the Windham School District within the Texas Department of Criminal Justice.

A RECURSIVE PROCESS OF CHANGING PARADIGMS IN DOCTORIAL EDUCATION LEADERSHIP PROGRAMS

Betty Alford

> We are the dwelling place of incredible opportunities. They live within us.
>
> —John Denver (in Blaydes, 2003, p. 20)

As I drove to the university to teach a Saturday 8:00 a.m. educational leadership doctoral class, I realized I was feeling lighthearted and energized, and the cause was not my second cup of coffee. In contemplating my mood, I recognized that, among other factors that motivate and energize me from time to time, I am profoundly motivated by hope and the possibility of a brighter future. As I mentally reviewed my upcoming plan to discuss various components of motivation in schools and the role of leadership in building commitment and motivation to achieve equity and excellence for all students, I paused, realizing again the importance of connecting theories with practice.

I decided that I would begin class by asking students to consider the factors that have motivated them to work toward excellence, to embark on a new project, or to journey in a new direction. Questions to consider would include the following: Is it pride in a job "well done" that motivates? Is it passionate interest in a topic and the joy of discovery? Is it the hope that an answer to a burning question may be found? It could be all of these factors or none. My own motivation to change, among other factors, has sometimes been kindled by the love of a family member, the inherent joy of self-satisfaction, a commitment to a cause larger than self, or even a fear of what will happen next if no actions are taken. However, regardless of the source of motivation for change, motivation for school improvement can be strengthened by the hope that the change will result in a desired future (Fullan, 2001).

THE SFA SCHOLAR-PRACTITIONER DOCTORAL PROGRAM

The theme of scholar-practitioner leadership was selected as the guiding vision with core values of advocacy, reflective practice, lifelong learning, and reciprocal learning as integral parts of the Stephen F. Austin State University doctoral program design. Through my ongoing participation in program development and implementation as professor, and now as chair of the department, I have served as a participant-observer in the doctoral program. In this role, I have conducted focus groups with the students to acquire their perspectives of the program's strengths and weaknesses that have contributed to their development as scholar-practitioner leaders. In addition, as a faculty member, I have reviewed the yearly portfolio presentations in which students discuss the themes emergent in their development. In teaching a synthesis course for the program designed to deepen conceptual understanding and to strengthen connections between knowledge gained and practice, I have also listened to the voices of students as they related their stories of growth in scholar-practitioner leadership. Additional insights about the program have been gained through two surveys of graduates as well as informal conversations with students at conferences and between classes. From these data sources, emergent themes have been identified that are common across the seven years of program implementation.

One of our students in the doctoral program poignantly captured the essence of the change in his personal growth as a scholar-practitioner leader with a "change to a sense of restored hope and an intense desire to provide that sense of hope to others." He expressed concern that African Americans are being "left behind" in the teaching profession and a desire to influence a positive change from the current status quo. He emphasized that the readings and dialogue throughout his participation in the doctoral program have made him more hopeful that he could impact change.

Another student shared a changing perspective of testing:

> Starratt (2004) stressed that educational leaders must bridge high-stakes testing with authentic learning. He challenged me to present students with opportunities that will help them look into their own lives, to examine the big picture and use the high standards as an excuse to make a difference in the future of the child. . . . Now, instead of stressful test preparation strategies, I praise students and encourage their great efforts. This helped the students to believe in themselves, which made all the difference in the test scores. It also provided them with a level of confidence during the actual test-taking day. When the results were published by the state, the students who were once labeled low-performing achieved the highest level of accountability rating in the state of Texas.

My own sense of hopefulness that the doctoral program positively impacts each student's philosophy and practice in shaping educational leadership paradigms has strengthened as students have expressed recurrent themes. In this chapter, I discuss and share student voices from the past seven years that resonate with these emergent themes: a greater sense of personal efficacy, an increased understanding of the importance of relationships and collaboration to the change process, a greater realization of the importance of critical inquiry and reflective-evaluative practices in achieving positive change, and a greater understanding of the importance of the leader's role as an advocate for students and social justice.

PERSONAL EFFICACY

Efficacy has been defined as an individual's judgment of his or her capacity to do whatever is necessary to attain desired results. Frequently, doctoral students express a feeling of greater confidence as a result of participation in doctoral classes in educational leadership. One student even pointed out, "This carries into my work. I have greater confidence now."

Another student added,

> When "No Child Left Behind" (NCLB) stipulated that students needed highly qualified teachers, our district had 48 uncertified instructional paraprofessionals working in the district. I worked collaboratively with others to design a plan to meet the NCLB standards. We shifted professional development funds to pay for college tuition and provided tuition assistance for the paraprofessionals to attend a neighboring community college. Three chose to leave the district, but of those who remained, only three are not now fully certified.

This student further emphasized, "Participation in a doctoral program taught us to ask questions and to take positive actions. I want you to know that results are being achieved from the efforts." Statements such as these suggest the deepened understanding of educational issues resulting from students' studies and a greater sense of efficacy in practice.

One student commented that he entered the program because he was on a statewide board with many urban superintendents who had completed doctoral degrees and "saw that they had a depth of understanding that I was lacking. This is what prompted me to join a doctoral program." In graduating, the same student expressed his increased "confidence in my knowledge and skills. I don't know all the answers, but I am not afraid of a challenge. I know how to research and where to go for support. I have deepened my understanding of educational issues, and this has impacted my leadership style."

This sense of efficacy is combined with a heightened sense of courage to "take a stand." Duffy (2003) suggests that leadership is not for the timid or fainthearted. As a student shared,

> Courage in the workplace is vital. Through the readings, I know I must develop a brave heart to maintain the level of high expectations in my school. I also understand the importance of having passion for my profession. I know that I must approach each day with passion in order to maintain the environment that is necessary for a positive school culture.

Another student added,

> I am much more aware of the dynamics that occur between the staff and faculty to the atmosphere of the school and the interrelationship to me as

the school leader. Being a doctoral student has heightened awareness, sparked campus reform, and given me strength to move in the direction that I inherently knew was right. My background knowledge has broadened tremendously.

In describing the transformation in leadership style, a student explained, "I have moved from a good technician to a quality leader with enhanced understanding of democracy and of growth in critical thinking. Through extensive reading and discussion, I have shifted in my leadership style to an ongoing recognition of life as research to encourage new ideas and new thoughts." This confidence in abilities as a strengthened sense of efficacy is embedded in a heightened awareness of the importance of collaborative processes and quality relationships in organizational improvements.

COLLABORATIVE PROCESSES AND RELATIONSHIPS

Through dialogue and discussion in doctoral classes in educational leadership, graduate students analyze leadership styles and collaborative processes. This leads to an enhanced understanding of the importance of collaborative processes in school improvement efforts. One student noted, "The way I lead our school's efforts to improve our accountability rating changed as a result of the program. From a role of an enforcer, I became a coach and an encourager of the process. As a result, we greatly improved our accountability scores."

Another student added,

> Being in a doctoral program has provided me an important groundwork for "true" collaborative practice within my school. The paper I just completed helps me to focus and understand just how imperative collaborative decision making truly is. In the past, my individual approach to leadership had been very autocratic. I have learned that the practices of relationship building, empowering, and giving voice to all stakeholders is an imperative in authentic leadership. I will take with me not only knowledge of collaboration but also a practice within the context of collaboration.

In the words of one of our students, "Strategic leaders build broad collaborative bases and lead with vision." Inherent in collaborative processes is the importance of trust. Donaldson (2001) maintains that collaboration is the glue that holds the organization together, and trust builds commitment to organizational change. As a student stressed, "I now spend much more time on establishing relationships. This means that my workday is often longer than before I entered the doctoral program because I spend more time building relationships." The student further added, "Relationships are the foundation change is built upon. When relationships improve, schools get better."

Students describe the cohort process as critical in their recognition of the importance of relationships. As a student stressed,

> I quickly realized the importance of my cohort members and the strong authentic relationships that we have forged. I genuinely believe that one of the strengths of this program is the cohort model and the strong friendships that emerge as we struggle to construct meaning in the scholar-practitioner role. In our readings, the importance of these affirming relationships was explored in detail. We were experiencing this power of relationships.

The power of relationships has built strength and conviction. A student shared, "Not only have we walked the fire of a doctoral residency together, [but] we have developed strength in our relationships that will last far beyond the stretch of our doctoral experience. I have a sense that this family-like bond, easily known to those of us who are living it, is something special that is not found often in life."

REFLECTIVE PRACTICE AND CRITICAL INQUIRY

Students further expressed the addition of heightened inquiry skills and reflective practice during and after participation in a doctoral program. For example, one student emphasized, "Now, if someone suggests a program for school adoption, I immediately do a computer search to learn more about the program. In reading the research reports and sharing the reports with others at my school, we are using research to guide practice." Another student added, "There were cases where I have read something that I have observed or struggled with on my campus professionally. I now have the beginnings of a theoretical foundation to give credibility when discussing educational issues on my campus." Further, a student emphasized,

> I have changed so much in all areas, professionally and personally. Because of the exposure to the writings and literature, I am able to define things in terms of what is effective and desirable in leadership, whether it is as a school administrator or just a leader of people. I have changed within my area of leadership at school. I have miles to go, but only I know how far I have come. I am more confident in my abilities to lead and much more willing to take risks.

Another student expressed, "We now conduct action research on our practices. We collect data to determine the results of our interventions and evaluative and discuss data in determining next steps."

Students also emphasized a strengthening of reflective practice as part of their educational leadership paradigm. As a student shared, "Now, I find myself constantly reflecting on my actions and writing in my educational journal." Growth in reflective practice, in critical analysis, and in practical application was clearly illustrated throughout by a student's comment of appreciation of the "awesome opportunity to think at higher levels." Another student added, "Scholar-practitioner leadership is a pathway that is guided by reflection and inquiry, not a static goal."

ADVOCACY FOR SOCIAL JUSTICE

Students also expressed an increased awareness of social justice and a stronger recognition of the importance of advocacy for student success. They expressed a heightened consciousness of the need for social justice as a leadership attribute in schools. Questioning and researching the current system as to its effect on all individuals were cited as important components of scholar-practitioner leadership. Students' comments serve as poignant reminders of the importance of nurturing growth through an enriching environment that stimulates learning. For example, a student stressed, "I now wonder when I decided to drop out of a specialized academic-intensive program in New York why no one encouraged me to stay. What did I know as a fifth-grade African American student of the importance of this opportunity to my later success?"

A growing awareness of issues of social justice has influenced positive actions by students. A student stressed,

> At one point, I experienced an epiphany when I realized through the use of self-reflection that as a leader, I must be careful that cultural capital is not used by the more powerful segments in society to depress the rights and privileges of certain marginalized groups. I became aware of how the European American population uses its resources, language usage, and cultural knowledge to create dual educational systems for culturally diverse populations. I realized that I must commit to the virtues of courage, justice, and faith out of a critical and transformational spirit. As an educational leader, I am going to make sure that I take actions that are based on social justice and equity.

Another student echoed this commitment to social justice principles:

> As I opened my eyes to those around me, it not only became clear to me that there was dominant culture but it also became clear that I was a part of it. My whole perspective had changed. I read the *Pedagogy of the Oppressed* again. This time, I read it with a new appreciation. This experience has greatly benefited me in my practice. As I became more culturally sensitive and fought harder for social justice, I saw the improvement of the students of my school.

Another student traced his journey to a new worldview, stating,

> As a community member, I have become much more aware and vocal of social justice issues. I now see poverty and race in a new light. The book that has impacted me the greatest would have to be Margaret Wheatley's *Leadership and the New Sciences*. This book made me go back and look at the way I treat others and build relationships with my staff, students, and family members. Another text that greatly impacted my practice is Paulo Freire's *Pedagogy of the Oppressed*. This book caused me to rethink the issues of dignity, justice, and to some extent democracy. Duffy's book, *Courage, Passion, and Vision*, gave me just what the title states. I now seize opportunities with purpose and focus.

DISCUSSION

Students' doctoral experiences serve as a catalyst for lifelong learning. Their questions, their reflections, and their experiences make each course new and serve as evidence that our work matters. Their evaluative comments provide hope and assurance that these scholar-practitioner leaders are serving as transformational leaders in schools. Recently, a student commented on his "resolve to make a positive difference." Another student responded, "Although the process of growth will continue for the rest of my life, it has been a joy to discover that my potential is not limited. I am an unfinished product!" One student commented after a presentation by Robert J. Starratt, "As Starratt shared, we are all in the process of 'becoming.' After all, the world has 'waited thousands of years for us.' I look forward to the continuation of the process." Yet another student expressed, "I look forward to future growth and courage as I not only generate new scholarship, but have the courage to put my knowledge into action as a scholar-practitioner."

Participating in a doctoral program does not identify a magic bullet for students' leadership styles. Primarily, programs such as this reinforce the value of hard work and critical inquiry. Student comments articulate ways that participating in a doctoral program make a positive difference in their educational leadership paradigms. Their comments serve as testimony to the hope and the promise of a future wherein educational leaders do, indeed, serve as models of important leadership practices and processes in the transformation of schools for improved learning for all.

Betty Alford is associate professor and department chair of the Department of Secondary Education and Educational Leadership at Stephen F. Austin State University in Nacogdoches, Texas.

18

CHANGING MINDSETS OF EDUCATIONAL LEADERS

Sandra Harris

We must be the change we wish to see in the world.

—Mahatma Gandhi (in Blaydes, 2003, p. 85)

As suggested by the 2001 National Commission for the Advancement of Educational Leadership Preparation (NCAELP), doctoral programs in educational leadership are at a crossroads of change. Just as the Chinese proverb reminds us that "a journey of a thousand miles must begin with a single step," the journey to reenvision and rebuild leadership programs is in progress. There are more leadership doctoral programs throughout the country and the world than ever before, which means that more students than ever are participating in this journey of continued lifelong formal learning. Increasingly, the possession of an earned doctoral degree opens doors for enhanced professional opportunities for educators.

Many new and revised older doctoral programs are scholar-practitioner programs in educational leadership. These scholar-practitioner programs are generally identified by certain components, such as problem-based learning, using a cohort model, forging collaborative relationships with school districts, and including field-based internships. Another major emphasis of scholar-practitioner doctoral programs is that of merging theory and practice rather than maintaining them as two separate entities. But most importantly, there is an emphasis on school improvement, democratic community, and social justice (Murphy, 2001). Therefore, the goal of scholar-practitioner graduate programs is transformative in nature, indicating that they are grounded in the study of the realities of leadership and are consistently engaging in inquiry. This suggests that learning is problem based and learners are "engaged in making meaning about their social world" (Anderson & Saavedra, 2001, p. 1).

Learning is a wonderful thing. But learning in isolation of changing behavior and changing practices is meaningless. Certainly university graduate educational leadership programs that are restructuring to build programs that connect scholarly learning and theory with the practice of improving schools are on the right track. But all programs are limited by one fundamental concept: goals and aspirations of the learner. This leads to the suggestion that true learning that transforms practice is driven by the heart and soul of the learner's personal/professional goals. Peter Senge notes that when programs fail "to tap the power of aspiration, deep learning and change are virtually impossible" (Spears, 2002, p. 349).

All of this leads to the dual question that all doctoral programs should ask: As students learn about leadership, does their practice change? If so, does this changing practice result in school improvement?

STUDY SETTING

The 16 students whose essays are included in this book were nearly halfway through completion of a doctoral scholar-practitioner program when these were written. They had completed 24 hours of core doctoral classes and were enrolled in a summer session that consisted of a field internship and a seminar synthesis class. Throughout the coursework, educational theories that covered a wide expanse of learning emphasizing school improvement through social justice had been discussed.

Discussion also focused on the actual practice of education. Class discussions often emphasized what education theories looked like when implemented on the school campus. In the beginning of their doctoral work, students held class discussions that often distinctly separated theory and practice. In other words, scholarly discussions centered on theory in a broad, universal context, and then practical discussions followed emphasizing what was actually happening in schools.

However, as students became immersed in a variety of scholarly and practitioner readings, conversations began to integrate with practice and discussions of practice began to integrate with theory. The quality of the cohort dialogue grew from either one of scholarly theory or one of practice, to dialogue that integrated theory and practice. By the summer when students began writing their synthesis papers to address their changing mindsets or understandings of leadership and what this looked like, the practitioner had become so infused with the scholar and the scholar so infused with the practitioner that on most occasions, dialogue was that of a scholar-practitioner.

When students presented the synthesis paper in an oral presentation, their stories resonated with how their professional and personal lives had been changed. With every presentation, the emotion in the room was palpable. Listeners were frequently moved to tears as students described life-changing experiences. Occasionally, the students who were presenting were so overcome with emotion that their voices would break, or they would pause a moment before continuing.

USE OF METAPHOR

As I read the student papers and listened to their presentations, many of the students described their learning through metaphor. This in itself is a reflection of the effect of a scholar-practitioner approach to learning. As Beck (2000) explains, education as a field of scholarship and practice was built heavily on objectivist presumptions that sought precise, unambiguous definitions of discreet variables. However, today these approaches must be "supported, guided, and informed by an appreciation of the ways imagination, images, and metaphors both reflect and shape our worlds and work" (p. 41). Metaphors are powerful forces that use creative language and current understandings to synthesize new learning and experiences into deeper, more relevant understandings that profoundly influence our actions. Thus, students described the learning and changing that was occurring in their lives using rich visual metaphors, such as Moses on Mt. Sinai, Dorothy in the *Wizard of Oz*, a sorority/fraternity pledge line, and the metamorphosis of a butterfly to clarify how continued ongoing learning was impacting their practice.

DOES PRACTICE CHANGE AND DOES IT LEAD TO SCHOOL IMPROVEMENT?

Through metaphor and through describing critical incidents in their lives professionally and personally, four themes emerged that suggest that understandings of leadership practice do indeed change and that in doing so, doctoral students become more equipped to lead school improvement. These themes are

- Struggling to increase personal capacity
- Recognizing the need for authenticity
- Nurturing an enhanced sensitivity to others
- Embracing the unfinishedness of learning

Struggling to Increase Personal Capacity

Several of the students wrote and spoke about "doubts and uncertainties" at being successful in a doctoral program, as well as their fears that they could not bring about school improvement. Yet despite their "feeling very small," their desire to continue learning, to expand their experiences, to bring more "significance to their life," they persevered in the program and at their schools. In this way they also realized that their personal capacity for learning, for new experiences, and for influencing schools was growing far greater than they had imagined.

Students also pointed out that despite the direction from readings, professors, and ongoing dialogue, they had to "take a stand based on [our] own perception of these beliefs and values." This required courage. Through building relationships with other cohort members and through growing understandings of the power of dialogue and reflection, their capacity for courage increased. The struggle to increase personal capacity resulted in a changing dynamic understanding of their own potential capacity to learn more and do more.

Acknowledging the Need for Authenticity

Authenticity begins when we understand who we are and the importance of our "walk matching our talk." For example, one student realized that to truly be an authentic leader who cared for all students, she must do something at her school to connect education with career awareness. Several doctoral students wrote about the importance of authentic leaders equipping teachers to be empowered.

Other students wrote about the dilemma of having an authentic concern for students to be successful and the current emphasis on standardized testing in our nation. In each case, these doctoral students began changing their approach to testing because of its effect on students. Acknowledging the need for authenticity as a leadership construct impacted student practice by emphasizing responsibility for public actions that matched private and public dialogue of valuing others.

Nurturing an Enhanced Sensitivity to Others

In talking about deeper understandings of others, nearly every student emphasized an almost spiritual zeal to build better, stronger, more caring relationships with others of all ages and all backgrounds. As one student wrote, "I must uncover the distortions that exist in our language and our view of the world. . . . If I am truly committed to children, then I must critique the present order and I must believe that change is possible." Another said it this way: "A question that I must face now and in the future becomes, How can I establish an environment in my school that facilitates every person being given an equitable, fair, respectful, and just opportunity to achieve, with pride, his or her greatest potential?"

One student described the changes that she helped initiate for the school district to become inclusionary. Another pointed out how her greater understanding, and awareness in general, went beyond the students in her school to helping parents who were in need.

Becoming sensitive to others speaks the "true essence of why I teach," wrote one student, as he explained how he had come to understand that "teaching is not about me; it is about the students." Another student became acutely aware of her responsibility to help create students who are "dreamers of possible utopias." In this time of change when our world has become smaller and smaller through travel, media, and other technological advances, our sensitivity for others must be nurtured to become greater and wiser in order to improve schools for a widely diverse population.

Embracing the "Unfinishedness" of Learning

Nearly every student wrote about his or her awareness of the "unfinishedness" of learning. In other words, through learning, students became more understanding of the richness inherent in learning itself. This very process of identifying that they would always be unfinished served as a catalyst to continue learning, not so that they could finally learn everything there was to know . . . but to embrace the mystery that there would always be more to know. This constantly motivates students to look ahead with eagerness and excitement to what the future holds as they "chisel out" a vision that encompasses all learners. As student leadership mindsets changed regarding knowledge, the students' ever-growing capacities for diverse experiences also increased.

CONCLUSION

The student writers of these essays were educators who aspired to participate in deep learning with the goal of improving schools through their leadership. Their stories describe how good educators become even better educators; how they bring about change to a school; how they become more caring, more intuitive to campus needs, more sensitive to the moral and ethical dilemmas of schooling, and more welcoming of diversity; and how they draw on a renewed sense of spirituality, learn to be more empowering, and develop a renewed understanding of teacher-leaders.

In the past, policy makers have decried the lack of "modern content and clinical experiences" in educational leadership programs (Milstein & Krueger, 1997, p. 101). But the messages in these essays suggest that educational leadership programs can meet the challenge for programs to enfold the study of democratic community and social justice within the school improvement paradigm. When university doctoral programs incorporate field experiences, implement the cohort model, merge theory and practice, and focus on curriculum that emphasizes democratic community and social justice, school improvement occurs. However, these changing understandings of leadership and the resultant school improvements are certainly not isolated to this one university experience. On the contrary, leadership learning experiences shared in this book are occurring in scholar-practitioner programs across the United States. As doctoral students learn about leadership within settings such as this, their practice is changing, and this changing leadership practice is resulting in school improvement.

In the movie *Dead Poets Society*, the teacher, John Keating, challenges his classroom of young boys, "Words and ideas can change the world." A doctoral program in educational leadership has the potential to change the world. It does this by changing mindsets to struggle to increase personal capacity, to acknowledge the need for authenticity, to nurture an enhanced sensitivity to others, and to embrace our "unfinishedness." The quest for a doctoral degree is rigorous, both personally and professionally, and the goal of improving our schools is worthy. Yet the opportunity to change the world is a real possibility that begins when we change ourselves, and then our schools.

Sandra Harris is associate professor of educational leadership and director of the Center for Research and Doctoral Studies in Educational Leadership at Lamar University in Beaumont, Texas.

REFERENCES

REFERENCES

Anderson, G. (1998). The cultural politics of schools: Implications for leadership. *American Educational Research Journal*, 35(4), 947–962.

Anderson, G. L., & Saavedra, E. (2003). School-based reform, leadership, and practitioner research: Mapping the terrain. *Scholar-Practitioner Quarterly*, 1(1), 23–38.

Barth, R. S. (1990). *Improving schools within*. San Francisco: Jossey-Bass.

Barth, R. S. (2002). The culture builder. *Educational Leadership*, 59(8), 6–11.

Beals, M. P. (1995). *Warriors don't cry*. New York: Pocket Books.

Beck, L. G. (2000). Behind the scholarship, below the practice lie metaphors . . . and we need to pay attention to them. *Journal for the Scholar-Practitioner Leader*, 1(1), 39–52.

Bennett, L., Jr. (2000). *Forced into glory: Abraham Lincoln's white dream*. Chicago: Johnson.

Berger, A. (1995). *Cultural criticism*. London: Routledge.

Blaydes, J. (2003). *The educator's book of quotes*. Thousand Oaks, CA: Corwin Press.

Bolman, L. G., & Deal, T. E. (2001). *Leading with soul: An uncommon journey of spirit*. San Francisco: Jossey-Bass.

Bracken, B. A., & McCallum, R. S. (1998). *Nonverbal assessment of intelligence: Introduction to the unit, Universal Nonverbal Intelligence Test.*. Boston: Riverside.

REFERENCES

Bryk, A., & Schneider, B. (2003). Trust in schools: A core resource for school reform. *Educational Leadership*, 60(6), 40–44.

Bullard, P., & Taylor, B. (1993). *Making school reform happen*. Boston: Allyn & Bacon.

Cook, J. (1997). *The book of positive quotations*. Minneapolis, MN: Fairview Press.

Dantley, M. E. (2003). Principled, pragmatic, and purposive leadership: Reimagining educational leadership through prophetic spirituality. *Journal of School Leadership*, 13(2), 181–197.

Deal, T. E., & Kennedy, A. A. (1982). *Corporate cultures: The rites and rituals of corporate life*. Reading, MA: Addison-Wesley.

Dewey, J. (1916). *Democracy and education: An introduction to the philosophy of education*. New York: Free Press.

Dillon, S. (1994, April 7). Special education soaks up New York's school resources. *New York Times*, p. 18.

Donaldson, G. (2001). *Cultivating leadership in schools: Connecting people, purpose, and practice*. New York: Teachers College Press.

Doyle, L. H., & Doyle, P. M. (2003). Building schools as caring communities: Why, what, and how? *Clearing House*, 76(5), 259–261.

Duffy, F. (2003). *Courage, passion, and vision: A guide to leading systemic school improvement*. Lanham, MD: Scarecrow Press.

Duignan, P., & Bhindi, N. (1997). Authenticity in leadership: An emerging perspective. *Journal of Educational Administration*, 35(3), 195–209.

Emerson, R. W. (2004). Emerson quotes. Transcendentalists. Retrieved August 23, 2004, from http://www.transcendentalists.com/emerson_quotes.htm.

Foster, W. (1994). School leaders as transformative intellectuals: Toward a critical pragmatism. In N. Prestine & P. Thurston (Eds.), *Advances in educational administration: Vol. 3. New directions in educational administration: Policy, preparation, and practice* (pp. 29-50). Greenwich, CT: Jai Press.

Freire, P. (1993). *Pedagogy of the oppressed*. New York: Continuum.

Freire, P. (1998). *Pedagogy of freedom: Ethics, democracy, and civic courage*. Lanham, MD: Rowman & Littlefield.

Freire, P. (2001). *Pedagogy of freedom: Ethics, democracy, and civic courage*. Lanham, MD: Rowman & Littlefield.

Fuchs, D., & Fuchs, L. S. (1995). What's special about special education? *Phi Delta Kappan*, 76, 522–530.

Fullan, M. (2001). *Leading in a culture of change*. San Francisco: Jossey-Bass.

Fullan, M. (2002). The change leader. *Educational Leadership*, 59(8), 16–20.

Fullan, M. (2003). *The moral imperative*. Thousand Oaks, CA.: Corwin Press.

Gardner, H. (1999). *Intelligence reframed: Multiple intelligences for the 21st century*. New York: Basic Books.

Giroux, H. (1994). Educational leadership and school administrators: Rethinking the meaning of democratic public cultures. In T. A. Mulkeen, N. H. Cambron-McCabe, & B. J. Anderson (Eds.), *Democratic leadership: The changing context of administrative preparation* (pp. 31–47). Norwood, NJ: Ablex.

Gladwell, M. (2000). *The tipping point: How little things make a big difference.* New York: Little, Brown.

Greenfield, W. (1987). Moral imagination and interpersonal competence: Antecedents to instructional leadership. In W. D. Greenfield (Ed.), *Instructional leadership: Concepts, issues, and controversies* (pp. 143–169). Boston: Allyn & Bacon.

Groves, P. (2002). Doesn't it feel morbid here? High-stakes testing and the widening of the equity gap. *Educational Foundations, 16*(2), 15–28.

Handy, C. (1993). *Understanding organizations* (4th ed.). London: Penguin.

Harris, S. (2004). *Bravo principal: Building relationships with actions that value others.* Larchmont, NY: Eye on Education.

hooks, B. (2000). *Where we stand: Class matters.* New York: Routledge.

Howe, W. (1995). Leading with soul: An uncommon journey of spirit. *Business Horizons, 38*(1), 78–80.

Hoyle, J. (2002). *Leadership and the force of love.* Thousand Oaks, CA.: Corwin Press.

Jackson, B., & Kelley, C. (2001). *Exceptional and innovative programs in educational leadership.* Retrieved October 28, 2004, from http://www.NCAELP.org.

Jenlink, P. (2001, April). *Scholar-practitioner leadership: A critical analysis of preparation and practice.* Paper presented at the annual meeting of the American Educational Research Association, Seattle, WA.

Jordan, J. (1999). *The musician's soul: A journey examining spirituality for performers, teachers, composers, conductors, and music educators.* Chicago: GIA Publications.

Kessler, R. (1999). Nourishing students in secular schools. *Educational Leadership, 56*(4), 49–52.

Kidder, R. (2002). Moral courage in a world of dilemmas. *School Administrator, 59*(2), 10–15.

Kidder, R. M. (1996). *How good people make tough choices: Resolving the dilemmas of ethical living.* New York: Simon & Schuster.

Kincheloe, J. L., & Steinberg, S. R. (1999). A tentative description of post-formal thinking: The critical confrontation with cognitive theory. In J. L. Kincheloe, S. R. Steinberg, & P. H. Hinchey (Eds.), *The post-formal reader: Cognition and education* (pp. 55–90). New York: Falmer Press.

REFERENCES

Kouzes, J. M., & Posner, B. Z. (2003). *Encouraging the heart: A leader's guide to rewarding and recognizing others.* San Francisco: Jossey-Bass.

Lawrence, W., Jones, E., & Smith, F. (1999). Students' perceived needs as identified by students. *Journal of Instructional Psychology, 26*(1), 22–29.

Lipsky, D. K., & Garner, A. (1987). Capable of achievement and worthy of respect: Education for handicapped students as if they were full-fledged human beings. *Exceptional Children, 54,* 69–74.

Littrell, J., & Peterson, J. (2001). Transforming the school culture: A model based on an exemplary counselor. *Professional School Counseling, 4*(5), 310–319.

Maxwell, J. C (1999). *The 21 indispensable qualities of a leader.* Nashville, TN: Thomas Nelson.

Maxwell, J. C. (2004). *The power of one: One person, one rule, one month.* Nashville, TN: Nelson Books.

Milstein, M. M., & Krueger, J. A. (1997). Improving educational administration preparation programs: What we have learned over the past decade. *Peabody Journal of Education, 71*(2), 100–116.

Moulton, J. (1924). Law and manners. *Atlantic Monthly, 134*(1), 1–5.

Mullen, C. A. (2003, November). *Informal doctoral mentoring cohorts: A creative response to barriers in leadership preparation.* Paper presented at the annual University Council of Educational Administrators (UCEA) in Portland, OR.

Murphy, J. (1992). *The Landscape of leadership preparation: Reframing the education of school administrators.* Newbury Park, CA: Corwin Press.

Murphy, J. (1999). *The quest for a center: Notes on the state of the profession of educational leadership.* Columbia, MO.: University Council for Educational Administration.

Murphy, J. (2001). *Reculturing the profession of educational leadership: New blueprints.* Retrieved October 28, 2004, from http://www.NCAELP.org.

Murphy, J. (2002). Reculturing the profession of educational leadership: New blueprints. *Educational Administration Quarterly, 38*(2), 176–191.

Noddings, N. (1999). *Justice and caring: The search for common ground in education.* New York: Columbia University Teachers College.

Nomura, K. (1999). Learning to lead. *Thrust for Educational Leadership, 29*(1), 18–20.

Nyquist, J. D., & Woodford, B. J. (2000). *Re-envisioning the Ph.D.: What concerns do we have?* Seattle: Center for Instructional Development and Research and University of Washington.

Oladele, F. (1999). Passing down the spirit. *Educational Leadership, 56*(4), 62–65.

Palmer, P. J. (1990). *The active life: A spirituality of work, creativity, and caring*. San Francisco: Jossey-Bass.

Payne, R. (1998). *A framework for understanding poverty*. Highlands, TX: RFT Publishing.

Perez, S. A. (2000). An ethic of caring in teaching culturally diverse students. *Education, 121*(1), 102–105.

Quantz, R. A., Rogers, J., & Dantley, M. (1991). Rethinking transformative leadership: Toward democratic reform of school. *Journal of Education, 173*(3), 97.

Rachels, J. (1993). *The elements of moral philosophy* (2nd ed.). New York: McGraw Hill.

Rachels, J. (2003). *The elements of moral philosophy* (4th ed.). New York: McGraw Hill.

Reynolds, A. J. (1991). Early schooling of children at risk. *American Educational Research Journal, 28,* 392–422.

Sergiovanni, T. J. (1992). *Moral leadership: Getting to the heart of school improvement*. San Francisco: Jossey-Bass.

Shapiro, J. P. (1993, December 13). Separate and unequal: How special education programs are cheating our children and costing taxpayers billions each year. *US News & World Report,* 46–49, 54–56, 60.

Short, P. M. (1994). Defining teacher empowerment. *Education, 114*(4), 488–493.

Short, P. M., & Rinehart, J. S. (1992). *The school participation empowerment scale*. Lexington, KY: Authors.

Sokolow, S. L. (2002). Enlightened leadership. *School Administrator, 8*(59), 32–36.

Solomon, J., & Hunter, J. (2002). A psychological view of spirituality and leadership. *School Administrator, 59*(8), 38–41.

Spears, L. C. (Ed.). (2002). *Servant leadership: A journey into the nature of legitimate power and greatness*. New York: Paulist Press.

Starratt, R. J. (1991). Building an ethical school: A theory for practice in educational leadership. *Educational Administration Quarterly, 27*(2), 185–202.

Starratt, R. J. (2004). The dialogue of scholarship. *Educational Administration Quarterly, 40*(2), 259–267.

Suhor, C. (1999). Spirituality—letting it grow in the classroom. *Educational Leadership, 56*(4), 12–16.

Tomlinson, C. (1999). *The differentiated classroom: Responding to the needs of all learners*. Alexandria, VA: Association for Supervision and Curriculum.

Valenzuela, A. (1999). *Subtractive schooling: U.S.-Mexican youth and the politics of caring*. Albany: State University of New York Press.

REFERENCES

Vasquez-Levy, D., & Timmerman, M. A. (2000). Beyond the classroom: Connecting and empowering teachers as leaders. *Teaching and Change, 7*(4), 363–371.

Wheatley, M. J. (1999). *Leadership and the new science: Discovering order in a chaotic world.* San Francisco: Berrett-Koehler.

Wheatley, M. J. (2002). Spirituality in turbulent times. *School Administrator, 59*(8), 42–46.

Wheatley, M. J., & Kellner-Rogers, M. (1999). *A simpler way.* San Francisco: Berrett-Koehler.

Williams, R. (1976). *Keywords.* London: Fontana.

Witcher, J. K. (2003). Ethical leadership: A promise to keep. *Delta Kappa Gamma Bulletin, 69*(3), 27–30.

RECOMMENDED READING

(This is a list of student-recommended readings.)

Barth, R. S. (2001). *Learning by heart.* San Francisco: Jossey-Bass.

Beck, L. G. (1994). *Reclaiming educational administration as a caring profession.* New York: Teachers College Press.

Burnham, J., & Jackson, C. (2000). School counselor roles: Discrepancies between actual practice and existing models. *Professional School Counseling, 4,* 41–49.

Chen, Da (1999). *Colors of the mountain.* New York: Random House.

Cherryholmes, C. (1998). *Power and criticism: Poststructural investigations in education.* New York: Teachers College Press.

Deal, T. E., & Peterson, K. D. (1999). *Shaping school culture: The heart of leadership.* San Francisco: Jossey-Bass.

Doyle, L. H., & Doyle, P. M. (2003). Building schools as caring communities: Why, what, and how? *Clearing House, 76*(5), 259–261.

Enderlin-Lampe, S. (2002). Empowerment: Teacher perceptions, aspirations and efficacy. *Journal of Instructional Psychology, 29*(3), 139–146. Retrieved October 8, 2003, from EBSCO host database.

Foster, W. (1994). School leaders as transformative intellectuals: Toward a critical pragmatism. *Advances in Educational Administration, 3,* 29–51.

Greenfield, T. B. (1984). Leaders and schools: Willfulness and nonnatural order in organizations. In T. J. Sergiovanni & J. E. Corbally (Eds.), *Leadership and organizational culture* (pp. 141–169). Chicago: University of Illinois Press.

Howard, G. R. (1999). *We can't teach what we don't know: White teachers, multiracial schools*. New York: Teachers College Press.

Johnson, S. (1998). *Who moved my cheese?* New York: G. P. Putnam's Sons.

Kahne, J. (1996). *Reframing educational policy: Democracy, community, and the individual*. New York: Teachers College Press.

Lewis, C. S. (1947). *The abolition of man: How education develops man's sense of morality*. New York: Macmillan.

Lundin, S. C., Paul, H., & Christensen, J. (2000). *FISH! A remarkable way to boost morale and improve results*. New York: Hyperion.

Maxwell, J. C. (1993). *Developing the leader within you*. Nashville, TN: Thomas Nelson.

Maxwell, J. C. (2000). *Failing forward: Turning mistakes into stepping stones for success*. Nashville, TN: Thomas Nelson.

Palmer, P. J. (1998). *The courage to teach: Exploring the inner landscape of a teacher's life*. San Francisco: Jossey-Bass.

Popkewitz, T. S. (1998). *Struggling for the soul: The politics of schooling and the construction of the teacher*. New York: Teachers College Press.

Sanborn, M. (2004). *The Fred factor*. New York: Doubleday.

Schlechty, P. C. (1997). *Inventing better schools: An action plan for educational reform*. San Francisco: Jossey-Bass.

Senge, P. M. (1990). *The fifth discipline: The art and practice of the learning organization*. New York: Doubleday.

Spring, J. (1994). *Wheels in the head: Educational philosophies of authority, freedom, and culture from Socrates to Paolo Freire*. New York: McGraw-Hill.

Spring, J. (1997). *Political agendas for education: From the Christian Coalition to the Green Party*. Mahwah, NJ: Lawrence Erlbaum.

Starratt, R. J. (1995). *Leaders with vision: The quest for school renewal*. Thousand Oaks, CA: Corwin Press.

Starratt, R. J. (2003). *Centering educational administration*. Mahwah, NJ: Lawrence Erlbaum.

Starratt, R. J. (2004). *Ethical Leadership*. San Francisco: Jossey-Bass.

Steinberg, S. R., Kincheloe, J. L., & Hinchey, P. H. (1999). A tentative description of post-formal thinking: The critical confrontation with cognitive theory. In S. R. Steinberg, J. L. Kincheloe, and P. H. Hinchey (Eds.), *The post-formal reader cognition and education* (pp. 56–90). New York: Falmer Press.

Sullivan, G. R., & Harper, M. V. (1997). *Hope is not a method*. New York: Broadway Books.

REFERENCES

U. S. Department of Education. (2002). *Career clusters: Focusing education on the future.* Washington, DC: Government Printing Office.

Warren, R. (2002). *The purpose driven life: What on earth am I here for?* Grand Rapids, MI: Zondervan

Wooden, J. R., & Jamison, S. (1997). *Wooden: A lifetime of observations and reflections on and off the court.* New York: Contemporary Books.

INDEX

Abrahams, Harold, 55
antiracism, 134
at-risk students, 5, 7, 77, 92, 93, 113, 120

Campus Placement Committee, 69
caring, 14, 24, 33, 45–46, 110, 114, 116, 124, 141–49, 161, 164; communities, 125–30; ethic of, 70, 71, 73, 90, 129
Carnegie unit, 53
change, viii, 32–34, 96–103, 155, 159, 160, 165; agent of, 85, 89; moment, 116; the world, 134, 165
chaos theory, 145
climate, 80
cohort dialogue, 161
cohort model, 108, 155, 159, 165
collaboration, v, 14, 30, 51, 72–73, 101, 118, 136, 152, 154, 155
community, 45, 71, 91, 95, 109, 122, 157; authentic learning, 115

confidence, 73, 74, 77–78, 153; lack of, 66, 67, 104, 107, 143
continuum of control, 101
corrective action plan, 85, 87
Cosby, Bill, 133
courage, 67, 72, 73, 107, 108, 110, 129, 132–34, 153; moral, 1–10, 26
critical inquiry, 72, 152, 155–56, 158
culture, 29–30, 32–35, 51, 106, 108; hip-hop, 137; limited experiences, 107
curriculum alignment, 101, 114

democracy, 4, 122, 157; democratic communitarian, 85; democratic values, 14, 18 160, 164
Dewey, John, 3, 12, 13, 14–15, 24
dilemma, mercy vs. justice, 7; moral, 3, 5, 6, 8; right vs. right, 6; right vs. wrong, 6

INDEX

discipline, classroom, 39–40; disciplinarian, 105; disciplinary action, 116
dissertation, vi, 49, 138

educational significance, 63, 64
empowerment, viii, 50, 76, 79, 81, 114, 146, 164; leader perception of, 79–80; student perception of, 76–77; teacher perception of, 77–78; teamwork of, 102
equity, 3, 8, 9, 14, 19, 26, 67, 83, 85, 94, 106, 126, 128, 135, 143, 150, 157
ethical leadership, 1, 3, 10

grace, 55–64

heart, 70–74, 115, 124, 160
high-stakes testing, 4, 7, 24–26, 35, 48, 89, 91, 114, 152
hope, 18, 19, 29, 40, 45, 46, 59, 63, 97, 117, 130, 148, 150, 151, 152, 158

Inclusion Project Grant, 91–94
inquiry skills, 155

justice, 26, 84, 122, 142; commitment to, 135

leadership, 23, 30–31, 146, 153, 154; authentic, 25, 27, 47, 73, 128, 132, 135–36, 143, 162, 163; authoritarian, 31; autocratic, 30; enlightened, 147; management, 145; transformational, 51, 54, 97, 158; visionary, 72
lifelong learning, 151, 158
love, 35, 37, 43, 48, 57, 93, 117, 125, 139, 143, 144, 151

Mann, Horace, 12
mentor, 7, 23, 46, 53, 79, 80, 106, 116, 135
metamorphosis, 123–30, 162
metaphor, 2, 67, 161–62
motivation, 59, 79, 116, 127, 142, 150–51
multiple intelligences, 88, 93, 145

namaste, 139
National Commission for the Advancement of Educational Leadership Preparation (NCAELP), vi, 159
National Commission on Excellence in Educational Administration, v
Newton, John, 60
No Child Left Behind Act, 153

Office of Civil Rights (OCR), 86–87

personal capacity, 162, 165
personal efficacy, 152–53
postformal perspective, 142
power 109, 145; coercive, 40; powerless, 1, 108
problem-based learning, 159
purpose, moral, 1, 5, 8, 15, 59, 84, 90, 94–95

reflection, vi, 3, 9–10, 11, 16–17, 18, 19, 43, 69, 74, 84–85, 89, 90, 97, 128, 131, 132, 137, 138, 143, 144, 146, 155–58, 161, 162
relationships, 11, 14, 17, 18, 19, 24, 27, 30, 33, 34, 43, 44, 56, 57, 69, 72, 90, 97, 102, 104, 112, 119, 127–29, 132, 135, 144, 152, 154–55, 157, 159, 162–63

INDEX

research, 14–16; using, 72
risk taking, vii, 33, 91, 127, 128

scholar-practitioner, vii, viii, 26, 68, 70, 85, 95, 109, 132, 134, 139, 148, 151–52, 156, 158, 159, 160, 161, 165
school improvement, vi, viii, 154, 160–65
schools: alienation toward, 62; career academies, 49–53; career education, 47–49; low-performing campus, 23, 26
self-actualize, 34
self-knowledge, 132, 134
sensitivity, 143, 162, 163–65
Site-Based Decision-Making Committee, 35
social injustice, 142
social justice, vii, viii, 3, 14, 67, 83, 85, 87, 94, 106, 110, 118, 126, 141–42, 152, 156–57, 160, 164, 165
Southern Association of Colleges and Schools (SACS) accreditation, 52
special education, 71; inclusion, 83–94; mainstreaming, 85
spiritual, 99, 124, 141–49; growth, 105, 106, 164; narrow definition, 142; spiritualize, capacity to, 56; transformative spiritual leaders, 143
staff training, 33, 69; teacher assistance, 91; team-building activities, 34
stereotypes, racial, 132
students: commitment to, 43, 46; culturally diverse, 70, 88, 90, 103, 110, 111, 119, 164
support systems, for parents and students, 117–18
systemic change, 50

tactical actions, 69
teacher-leaders, 11, 14, 15, 18, 19, 164
teaching: emptiness in, 43; first day of, 39–40
Texas Assessment of Knowledge and Skills (TAKS), 56, 94, 114
tipping points, 115–16
trust, 9, 17–19, 30, 33, 35, 42, 44, 51, 72, 78, 97, 98, 120, 136, 146, 148, 155

unfinishedness, 10, 81, 112, 120, 132, 158, 162, 164, 165

vision, 33, 114; common, 27